SCHOLASTIC

GRADES PreK-3

MARCH
Monthly Idea Book

Ready-to-Use Templates, Activities, Management Tools, and More—for Every Day of the Month

Karen Sevaly

New York • Toronto • London • Auckland • Sydney **Teaching**
Mexico City • New Delhi • Hong Kong • Buenos Aires *Resources*

- -

DEDICATION

This book is dedicated to teachers and children everywhere.

Cover design by Maria Lilja
Cover art by Jillian Phillips
Interior design by Melinda Belter
Illustrations by Karen Sevaly

ISBN 978-0-545-37939-7

2 3 4 5 6 7 8 9 10   40   19 18 17 16 15 14 13

CONTENTS

FAVORITE TOPICS

CONTENTS

JAPAN

WOMEN IN HISTORY

MARVELOUS MUSIC!

SPRING WEATHER

DOWN ON THE FARM

AWARDS, INCENTIVES, AND MORE

Reproducible Patterns

ANSWER KEY

INTRODUCTION

Welcome to the original Monthly Idea Book series! This book was written especially for teachers getting ready to teach topics related to the month of March.

Each book in this month-by-month series is filled with dozens of ideas for PreK–3 classrooms. Activities connect to the Common Core State Standards for Reading (Foundational Skills), among other subjects, to help you meet the needs of your students. (For more information, see page 16.)

Most everything you need to prepare the lessons and activities in this resource is included, such as:

- calendar and weather-related props
- book cover patterns and stationery for writing assignments
- booklet patterns
- games and puzzles that support learning in curriculum areas such as math, science, and writing
- activity sheets that help students organize information, respond to learning, and explore topics in a meaningful way
- patterns for projects that connect to holidays, special occasions, and commemorative events

All year long, you can weave the ideas and reproducible patterns in these unique books into your monthly lesson plans and classroom activities. Happy teaching!

What's Inside

You'll find that this book is
chock-full of reproducibles
that make lesson planning easier:

■ puppets and
picture props

■ bookmarks,
booklets, and
book covers

■ game boards,
puzzles, and
word finds

■ stationery

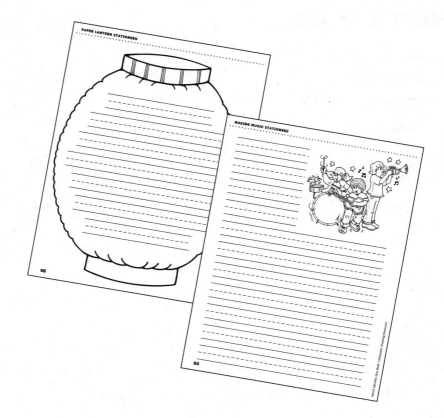

■ awards and certificates

How to Use This Book

The reproducible pages in this book have flexible use and may be modified to meet your particular classroom needs. Use the reproducible activity pages and patterns in conjunction with the suggested activities or weave them into your curriculum in other ways.

★ PHOTOCOPY OR SCAN

To get started, think about your developing lesson plans and upcoming bulletin boards. If desired, carefully remove the pages you will need. Duplicate those pages on copy paper, color paper, tagboard, or overhead transparency sheets. If you have access to a scanner, consider saving the pattern pages as PDF files. That way, you can size images up or down and customize them with text to create individualized lessons, center-time activities, interactive whiteboard lessons, homework pages, and more.

★ LAMINATE FOR DURABILITY

Laminating the reproducibles will help you extend their use. If you have access to a roll laminator, then you already know how fortunate you are when it comes to saving time and resources. If you don't have a laminator, clear adhesive vinyl covering works well. Just sandwich the pattern between two sheets of vinyl and cut off any excess. Then try some of these ideas:

- Put laminated sheets of stationery in a writing center to use for handwriting practice. Wipe-off markers work great on coated pages and can easily be erased with dry tissue.

- Add longevity to calendars, weather-related pictures, and pocket chart rebus pictures by preserving them with lamination.

- Transform picture props into flannel board figures. After lamination, add a tab of hook-and-loop fastener to the back of the props and invite students to adhere them to the flannel board for storytelling fun.

- To enliven magnet board activities, affix sections of magnet tape to the back of the picture props. Then encourage students to sort images according to the skills you're working on. For example, you might have them group images by commonalities such as initial sound, habitat, or physical attributes.

★ BULLETIN BOARDS

1. Set the Stage

Use background paper colors that complement many themes and seasons. For example, the dark background you used as a spooky display in October will have dramatic effect in November, when you begin a unit on woodland animals or Thanksgiving.

While paper works well, there are other background options available. You might also try fabric from a colorful bed sheet or gingham material. Discontinued rolls of patterned wallpaper can be purchased at discount stores. What's more, newspapers are easy to use and readily available. Attach a background of comics to set off a lesson on riddles, or use grocery store flyers to provide food for thought on a bulletin board about nutrition.

2. Make the Display

The reproducible patterns in this book can be enlarged to fit your needs. When we say enlarge, we mean it! Think BIG! Use an overhead projector to enlarge the images you need to make your bulletin board extraordinary.

If your school has a stencil press, you're lucky. The rest of us can use these strategies for making headers and titles.

■ Cut strips of paper, cloud shapes, or cartoon bubbles. They will all look great! Then, by hand, write the text using wide-tipped permanent markers or tempera paint.

■ If you must cut individual letters, use 4- by 6-inch pieces of construction paper. (Laminate first, if you can.) Cut the uppercase letters as shown on page 14. No need to measure, as somewhat irregular letters will look creative, not messy.

3. Add Color and Embellishments

Use your imagination! You'll be surprised at the great displays you can create.

- Watercolor markers work great on small areas. On larger areas, you can switch to crayons, color chalk, or pastels. (Lamination will keep the color off of you. No laminator? A little hairspray will do the trick as a fixative.)

- Cut character eyes and teeth from white paper and glue them in place. The features will really stand out and make your bulletin boards engaging.

- For special effects, include items that provide texture and visual interest, such as buttons, yarn, and lace. Try cellophane or blue glitter glue on water scenes. Consider using metallic wrapping paper or aluminum foil to add a bit of shimmer to stars and belt buckles.

- Finally, take a picture of your completed bulletin board. Store the photos in a recipe box or large sturdy envelope. Next year when you want to create the same display, you'll know right where everything goes. You might even want to supply students with pushpins and invite them to recreate the display, following your directions and using the photograph as support.

Staying Organized

Organizing materials with monthly file folders provides you with a location to save reproducible activity pages and patterns, along with related craft ideas, recipes, and magazine or periodical articles.

If you prefer, use file boxes instead of folders. You'll find that with boxes there will plenty of room to store enlarged patterns, sample art projects, bulletin board materials, and much more.

Meeting the Standards

CONNECTIONS TO THE COMMON CORE STATE STANDARDS

The Common Core State Standards Initiative (CCSSI) has outlined learning expectations in English/Language Arts, among other subject areas, for students at different grade levels. In general, the activities in this book align with the following standards for students in grades K–3. For more information, visit the CCSSI website at www.corestandards.org.

Reading: Foundational Skills

Print Concepts
- RF.K.1, RF.1.1. Demonstrate understanding of the organization and basic features of print.

Phonics and Word Recognition
- RF.K.3, RF.1.3, RF.2.3, RF.3.3. Know and apply grade-level phonics and word analysis skills in decoding words.

Fluency
- RF.K.4. Read emergent-reader texts with purpose and understanding.
- RF.1.4, RF.2.4, RF.3.4. Read with sufficient accuracy and fluency to support comprehension.

Writing

Production and Distribution of Writing
- W.3.4. Produce writing in which the development and organization are appropriate to task and purpose.
- W.K.5, W.1.5, W.2.5, W.3.5. Focus on a topic and strengthen writing as needed by revising and editing.

Research to Build and Present Knowledge
- W.K.7, W.1.7, W.2.7. Participate in shared research and writing projects.
- W.3.7. Conduct short research projects that build knowledge about a topic.
- W.K.8, W.1.8, W.2.8, W.3.8. Recall information from experiences or gather information from provided sources to answer a question.

Range of Writing
- W.3.10. Write routinely over extended time frames (time for research, reflection, and revision) and shorter time frames (a single sitting or a day or two) for a range of discipline-specific tasks, purposes, and audiences.

Speaking & Listening

Comprehension and Collaboration
- SL.K.1, SL.1.1, SL.2.1. Participate in collaborative conversations with diverse partners about grade-level topics and texts with peers and adults in small and larger groups.
- SL.K.2, SL.1.2, SL.2.2, SL.3.2. Recount or describe key ideas or details from a text read aloud or information presented orally or through other media.
- SL.K.3, SL.1.3, SL.2.3, SL.3.3. Ask and answer questions about what a speaker says in order to gather additional information or clarify something that is not understood.

Presentation of Knowledge and Ideas
- SL.K.4, SL.1.4, SL.2.4. Describe people, places, things, and events with relevant details, expressing ideas and feelings clearly.
- SL.K.5, SL.1.5, SL.2.5, SL.3.5. Add drawings or other visual displays to stories or recounts of experiences when appropriate to clarify ideas, thoughts, and feelings.

Language

Conventions of Standard English
- L.K.1, L.1.1, L.2.1, L.3.1. Demonstrate command of the conventions of standard English grammar and usage when writing or speaking.
- L.K.2, L.1.2, L.2.2, L.3.2. Demonstrate command of the conventions of standard English capitalization, punctuation, and spelling when writing.

Knowledge of Language
- L.2.3, L.3.3. Use knowledge of language and its conventions when writing, speaking, reading, or listening.

Vocabulary Acquisition and Use
- L.K.4, L.1.4, L.2.4, L.3.4. Determine or clarify the meaning of unknown and multiple-meaning words and phrases based on grade level reading and content, choosing flexibly from an array of strategies.
- L.K.6, L.1.6, L.2.6, L.3.6. Use words and phrases acquired through conversations, reading and being read to, and responding to texts.

CALENDAR TIME

Getting Started

March

Sunday	Monday	Tuesday	Wednesday	Thursday	Friday	Saturday

19

CALENDAR

★ MARK YOUR CALENDAR

Make photocopies of the calendar grid on page 19 and use it to meet your needs. Consider using the write-on spaces to:

- write the corresponding numerals for each day

- mark and count how many days have passed

- track the weather with stamps or stickers

- note student birthdays

- record homework assignments

- communicate with families about positive behaviors

- remind volunteers about schedules, field trips, shortened days, and so on

CELEBRATIONS THIS MONTH

Whether you post a photocopy of pages 20 through 23 near your class calendar or just turn to these pages for inspiration, you're sure to find lots of information on them to discuss with students. To take celebrating and learning a step further, invite the class to add more to the list. For example, students can add anniversaries of significant events and the birthdays of their favorite authors or historical figures.

CALENDAR HEADER

You can make a photocopy of the header on page 24, color it, and use it as a title for your classroom calendar. You might opt to give the coloring job to a student who has a birthday that month. The student is sure to enjoy seeing his or her artwork each and every day of the month.

BEFORE INTRODUCING WHAT'S THE WEATHER?

Make a photocopy of the body template on page 25. Laminate it so you can use it again and again. Before sharing the template with the class, cut out pieces of cloth in the shapes of clothing students typically wear this month. For example, if you live in a warm weather climate, your March attire might include shorts and t-shirts. If you live in chillier climates, your attire might include a scarf, hat, and coat. Fit the cutouts to the body outline. When the clothing props are made, and you're ready to have students dress the template, display the clothing. Invite the "weather helper of the day" to tell what pieces of clothing he or she would choose to dress appropriately for the weather. (For extra fun, use foam to cut out accessories such as an umbrella, sunhat, and raincoat.

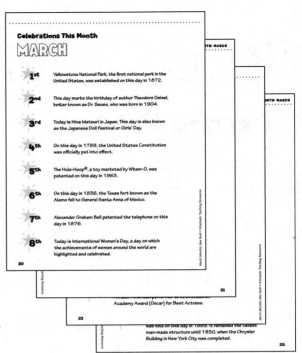

March

Sunday	Monday	Tuesday	Wednesday	Thursday	Friday	Saturday

Celebrations This Month

MARCH

1st Yellowstone National Park, the first national park in the United States, was established on this day in 1872.

2nd This day marks the birthday of author Theodore Geisel, better known as Dr. Seuss, who was born in 1904.

3rd Today is Hina Matsuri in Japan. This day is also known as the Japanese Doll Festival or Girls' Day.

4th On this day in 1789, the United States Constitution was officially put into effect.

5th The Hula-Hoop®, a toy marketed by Wham-O, was patented on this day in 1963.

6th On this day in 1836, the Texas fort known as the Alamo fell to General Santa Anna of Mexico.

7th Alexander Graham Bell patented the telephone on this day in 1876.

8th Today is International Women's Day, a day on which the achievements of women around the world are highlighted and celebrated.

9th The first Barbie™ doll made its debut at a toy fair in New York City on this day in 1959.

10th On this day in 1804, the United States doubled its size with a land acquisition known as the Louisiana Purchase.

11th Children's book author and illustrator Ezra Jack Keats was born on this day in 1916.

12th The Girl Scouts of the United States was founded on this day in 1912.

13th Uranus, the 7th planet from the Sun, was discovered on this day in 1781 by astronomer Sir William Herschel.

14th Albert Einstein, Nobel Prize winner and father of atomic energy, was born on this day in 1879.

15th On this day in 1985, symbolics.com became the world's first registered Internet .com-domain.

16th James Madison, fourth president of the United States, was born on this day in 1751.

17th Today is Saint Patrick's Day, a day that commemorates one of the patron saints of Ireland.

18th On this day in 1965, Soviet Cosmonaut Alexey Leonov became the first person to conduct a space walk.

19th Today, also known as Saint Joseph's Day, marks the annual "Return of the Swallows" to San Juan Capistrano. The swallows migrate to Argentina in October.

20th This day marks the first day of spring, which is also the vernal equinox—a day on which day and night are each approximately 12 hours long.

21st Today marks the birthday of German composer Johann Sebastian Bach, born in 1685.

22nd On this day in 1621, the Pilgrims signed a peace treaty with Massasoit, leader of the Wampanoags.

23rd World Meteorological Day is held annually on this day to focus international attention on weather and climate issues.

24th On this day in 2002, Halle Berry became the first African-American performer to be awarded an Academy Award (Oscar) for Best Actress.

25th Artist and sculptor Gutzon de la Mothe Borglum, creator of the famous Mt. Rushmore monument featuring four U.S. presidents, was born on this day in 1867.

26th Born on this day in 1930 was Sandra Day O'Connor, the first female to be appointed a Justice on the Supreme Court of the United States.

27th The Naval Act was passed by Congress on this day in 1794 to establish the first naval force of the United States of America.

28th Jesse Owens, winner of four gold medals in the 1936 Olympics, was awarded the Congressional Gold Medal on this date in 1990—almost ten years after his death.

29th On this day in 1929, President Herbert Hoover had a phone installed in the Oval Office of the White House. This was the first time a phone had been installed at the president's desk.

30th Dutch artist Vincent Van Gogh, creator of the famous Starry Night painting, was born on this day in 1853.

31st The dedication of the Eiffel Tower in Paris, France, was held on this day in 1889. It remained the tallest man-made structure until 1930, when the Chrysler Building in New York City was completed.

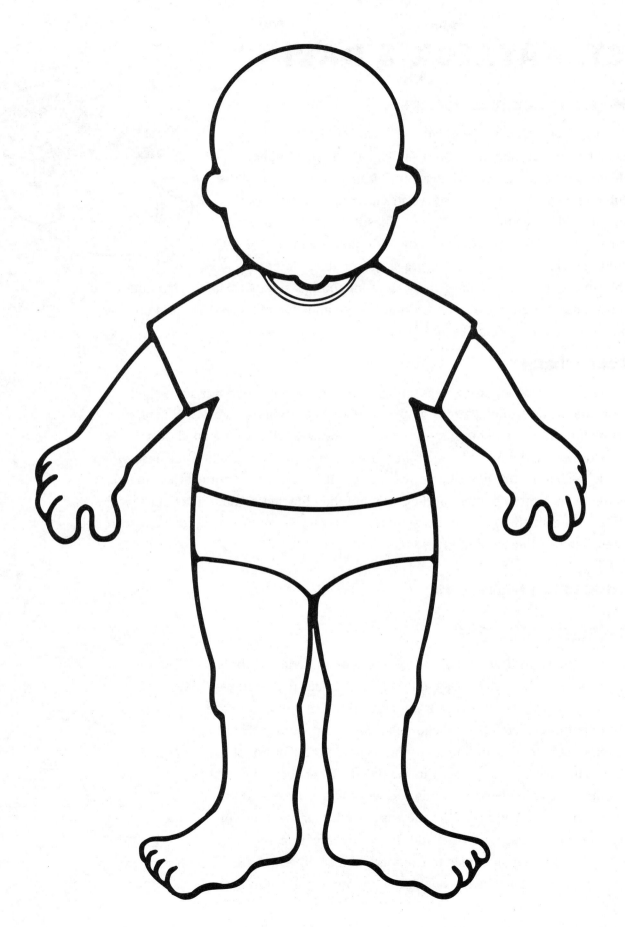

ST. PATRICK'S DAY!

Magonus Sucatus Patricius

Saint Patrick's Day is celebrated each year on March 17th to honor one of Ireland's patron saints, Saint Patrick. Most historians agree that Patrick was born around 385 A.D., that his full name was Magonus Sucatus Patricius, and that he was a member of a wealthy family. Legend has it that when he was a teenager, Patrick was kidnapped by Irish pirates and eventually sold as a slave. Most historians are skeptical about some of the stories credited to Saint Patrick. But one thing is sure: On March 17th, many folks around the world celebrate Saint Patrick and give him credit for bringing the shamrock plant to Ireland—and driving all the snakes away!

Leprechauns

Leprechauns are similar to elves and gnomes, but according to popular belief, leprechauns love to play tricks on people. One tale begins with an Irish gentleman who, after much searching, captured one of the wee folk. After a good deal of coaxing, the Irishman persuaded the leprechaun to take him to the very bush where the leprechaun's treasure of gold was buried. It is said that the quick-thinking man tied a red scarf to a branch on the bush and then hurried home to fetch a shovel. When the gentleman returned a short time later to dig up the treasure, a red scarf had been fastened to each and every bush in the forest!

Suggested Activities

 IRISH WORD FIND

Use the word find on page 31 to introduce students to words related to St. Patrick's Day and Ireland. Explain that each word in the puzzle reads across from left to right, or down from top to bottom (there are no diagonal or backward words). Then have students try to find all of the words in the word bank, circling each as they find it in the puzzle. After they complete the activity, review the words and work with students to define them. You might list the words and their meanings on chart paper. Also, you can add the words to your class word wall, and invite students to use them in a creative writing assignment, such as the one at the bottom of page 31.

★ ST. PATRICK'S DAY PICTURE PROPS

Copy, color, and cut out the patterns on pages 32–34. There are numerous uses for these, such as for nametags, calendar symbols, word walls, flash cards, patterning practice, or matching activities. Or, you might use an overhead projector to trace large images of the patterns onto poster board or bulletin board paper. Color, cut out, and use the images to create displays or signs to post around the room.

★ LUCKY LEPRECHAUN SKILLS WHEEL

Use the leprechaun wheel patterns on pages 35–36 to reinforce math skills and more. To prepare, write a problem in each of the large boxes (outlined in gray). Write the answer in the small box directly opposite each problem on the right. Cut out the leprechaun, pot of gold, and wheel. Then carefully cut out the "windows" on the leprechaun. Use one brass fastener to attach the wheel to the leprechaun and another to attach the pot of gold, as shown. To use, students turn to the wheel so that a problem appears in the left window. They solve the problem and then slide the pot of gold away from the right window to check their answer.

★ LEPRECHAUN COSTUME

Invite students to make the following props to prompt and enhance their learning about St. Patrick's Day and leprechauns. Students can wear the props to role-play leprechauns or to present their findings for the "Traditional Dress Puppets" activity on page 29.

Leprechaun Beard and Mustache

Distribute brown photocopies of the beard and mustache patterns (page 37) and have students cut them out. To wear, students loop the ends of the beard over their ears and use rolled tape to attach the mustache to their upper lip.

Leprechaun Ears

Photocopy a class set of the pair of ears (page 38) onto white construction paper. Invite students to color and cut out a pair of the ears. Have them fold each cutout back along the dashed line to form a tab, and then glue the ear-tabs to opposite sides of a sentence-strip headband (sized to fit the student's head).

Leprechaun Hat

Give each student a 6- by 22-inch sheet of green construction paper and a 14-inch green paper circle. Also, provide several tagboard copies of the hat buckle (page 38) and 6-inch tagboard circles for students to use as tracers. To make their leprechaun hats, have students do the following:

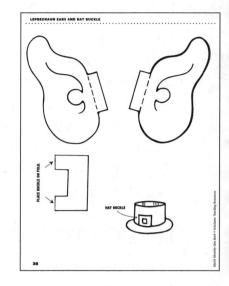

1. Tape the short ends of the green rectangle together to form a cylinder, as shown. This will be the tall part of the hat.

2. To make the brim, trace the 6-inch tagboard circle onto the center of the green circle. Cut out the smaller circle. Then cut notches around the inner circle, as shown.

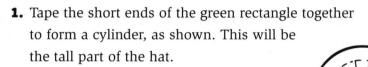

3. Fold up the notches in the brim and tape them to the inside of the hat.

4. For the hat buckle, fold a 2½ inch square of yellow construction paper in half. Trace the buckle tracer along the fold, then cut out the shape through both layers of paper. Unfold the buckle and tape (or glue) it to the hat.

★ FOLK-DANCER FINGER PUPPET

To make these finger puppets, photocopy one puppet pattern (page 39) for each student. Then have students color and cut out their puppet. Help them, as needed, to cut out the small circles on their puppet. To use, students slip their fingers into the holes and wiggle them around to serve as legs for their puppets. You might play a traditional Irish jig and invite students to "dance" their puppets around to the music.

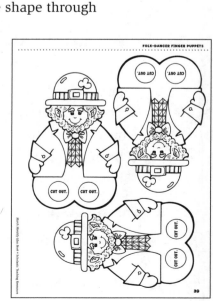

TRADITIONAL DRESS PUPPETS

Divide the class into several groups. Explain that each group will research different aspects of Irish life and then present their findings to the class. Assign one topic (such as food, clothing, shelter, industry, art, or transportation) to each group to research. Students can use books available in the classroom as well as library books, Internet resources, and other sources such as videos and personal interviews for their research. Tell groups that they should look for information about life in Ireland, both in the past and today, to compare how the people and culture have changed with the times. Younger students will enjoy hearing you read aloud from level-appropriate books on their topic. Afterward, they can discuss the information and then write and/or draw about what they have learned.

Most groups will need a few days to complete their research for this assignment. To help students prepare their presentations, provide copies of the puppet patterns on pages 40–41 for them to cut out, color, and embellish with craft items. For example, a student might glue cloth to their puppets to represent traditional formal dress. They can glue wide craft sticks to their puppets to serve as handles. To extend the activity, have groups create posters to show what they've learned about their particular topic. Then invite students to use their puppets and posters to present their findings to the class.

★ LUCKY LEPRECHAUN'S POT-O'-GOLD

Create your own game using this versatile game board. The game can be used for a small-group or learning-center activity. Or, make several games and divide the class into groups so they can all play at the same time! To get started, photocopy the game boards on pages 42–43. Glue the two parts of the game board together on poster board or to the inside of a file folder. How you use the game and which skills you want students to practice is up to you. Simply write the desired text (or problems) on the spaces of the game board and create task cards to use with the game. (You might use the flash cards on page 44 as task cards, if desired.) Then color the game board and cards, and laminate for durability.

★ SHAMROCK FLASH CARDS

Reinforce whatever your students are learning with flash cards that fit the theme of this unit. Simply photocopy the cards on page 44 and cut them apart. You can program the back of the cards for use as flash cards to teach:

- letters and numbers
- math facts
- content-area vocabulary words
- sight words

The cards are ideal for learning-center activities, but you might also use them to label job charts, group students, and more. To store, just put them in a resealable plastic bag.

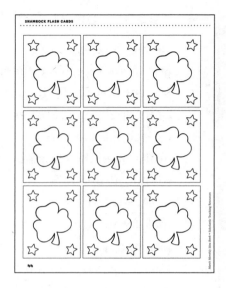

★ CLOVER STATIONERY

Liven up writing assignments with stationery ideal for writing about St. Patrick's Day, Irish culture, shamrocks, or any other related topic. Students might write poems, songs, acrostics, or imaginary stories. Distribute copies of the stationery on page 45 for students to use for their final drafts. Then invite volunteers to share their written work with the class.

★ WEE-FOLK BOOK COVER

For a finishing touch to students' March writing assignments or research projects, have them use the book cover on page 46. They can add a title and author line, color the art, and bind their written work behind the cover. When completed, invite students to share their work with classmates.

Irish Word Find

Find these words in the puzzle below:

BLARNEY   ERIN   FOLK   GAELIC   GNOME   IRELAND   JIG
LEPRECHAUN   SHAMROCK   SHENANIGAN   SHILLELAGH   WEE

```
A M S D F R E T G D F Q A S W D F R G B N M C D S J
A L C M A R Z H A C O V B G E N J X N E O U K I G A
L E S D E F R T G J L D S H E N A N I G A N I L I T
R P D S H A M R O C K R H G H Y J U K N O L G T D U
P R F G T H Y J U D F R I G H Y N J U O N H Y U G A
I E W E D C V G T D E B L A R N E Y R M T S W A W O
L C X C V B G F D S A W L R T G R A D E O F R S E Y
X H A F R E T Y H G T R E D C J I G R A X R G H J S
G A E L I C X M Z S E R L V G Y N Y A R E F G V B N
X U C V B G T A I R E L A N D E R K L E R A S E D F
A N S D F R C Y A S D C G F G D C V F G A U W U S T
A S X F E Y R X A R Y C H B H J K L O P M N G F D S
```

Using four of the words from the puzzle, write a paragraph about
Saint Patrick's Day. If you need more space to write, use the
back of this page.

_____

_____

_____

_____

_____

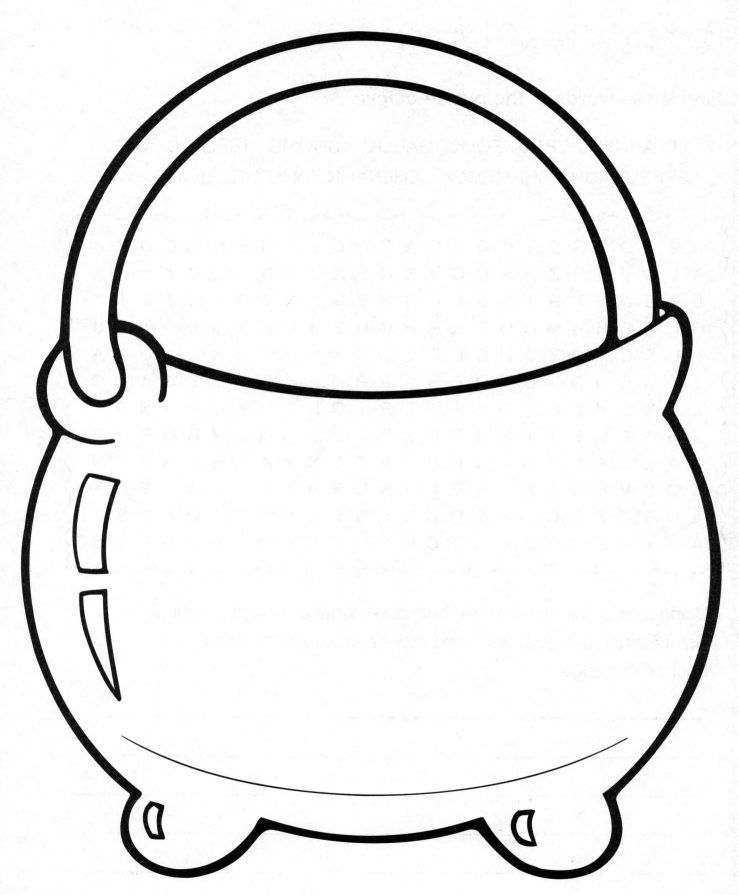

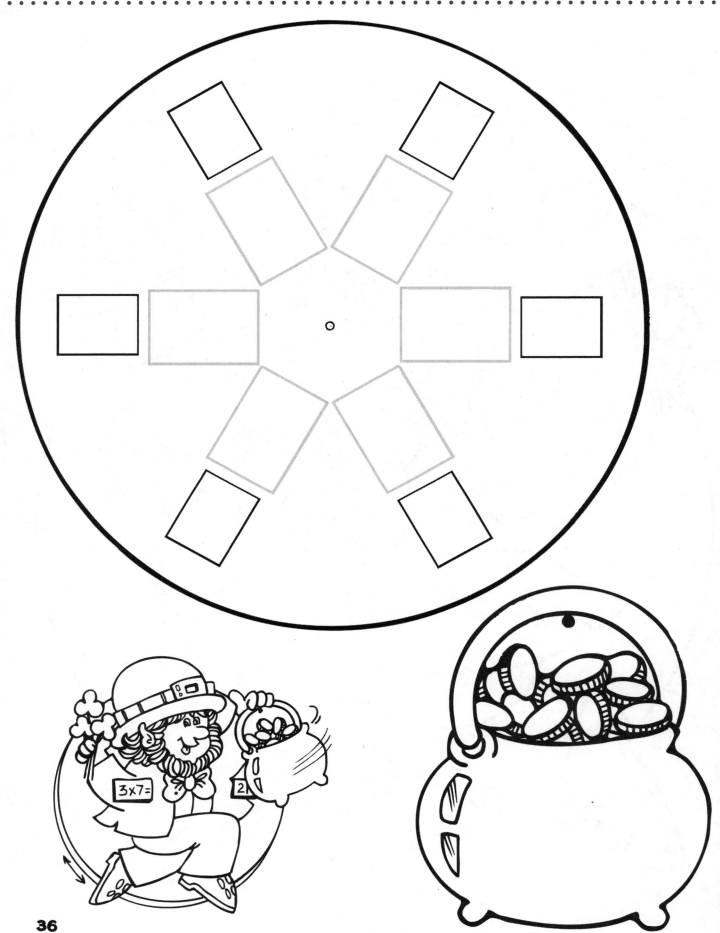

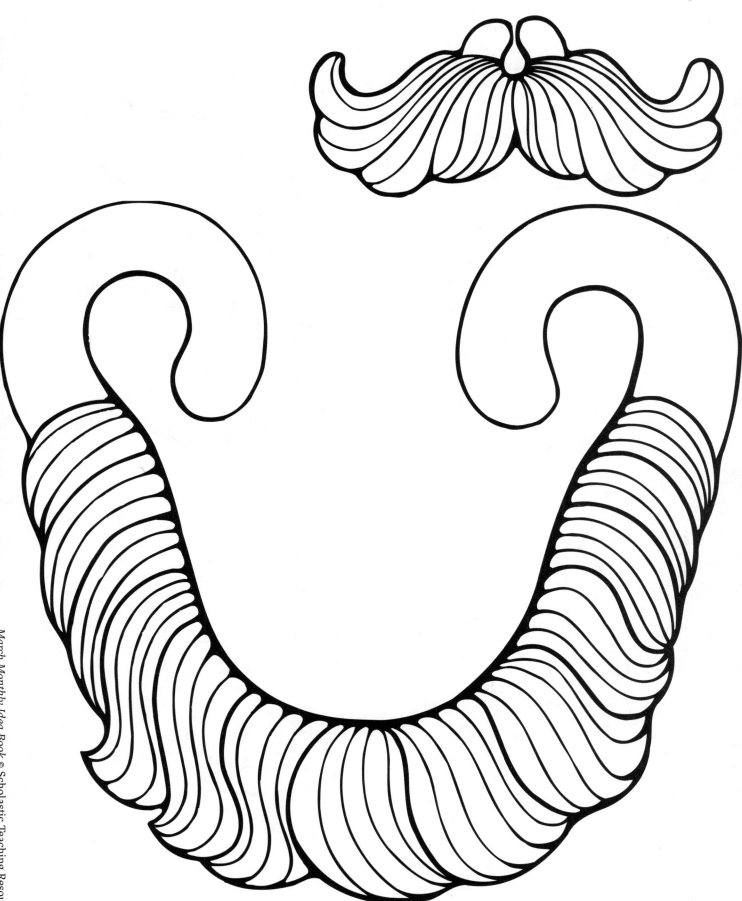

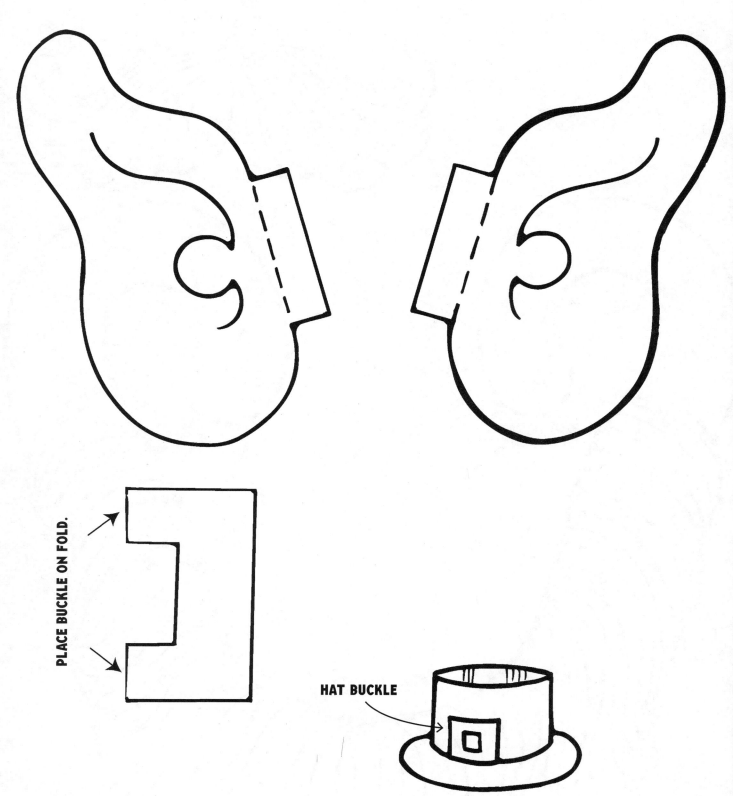

PLACE BUCKLE ON FOLD.

HAT BUCKLE

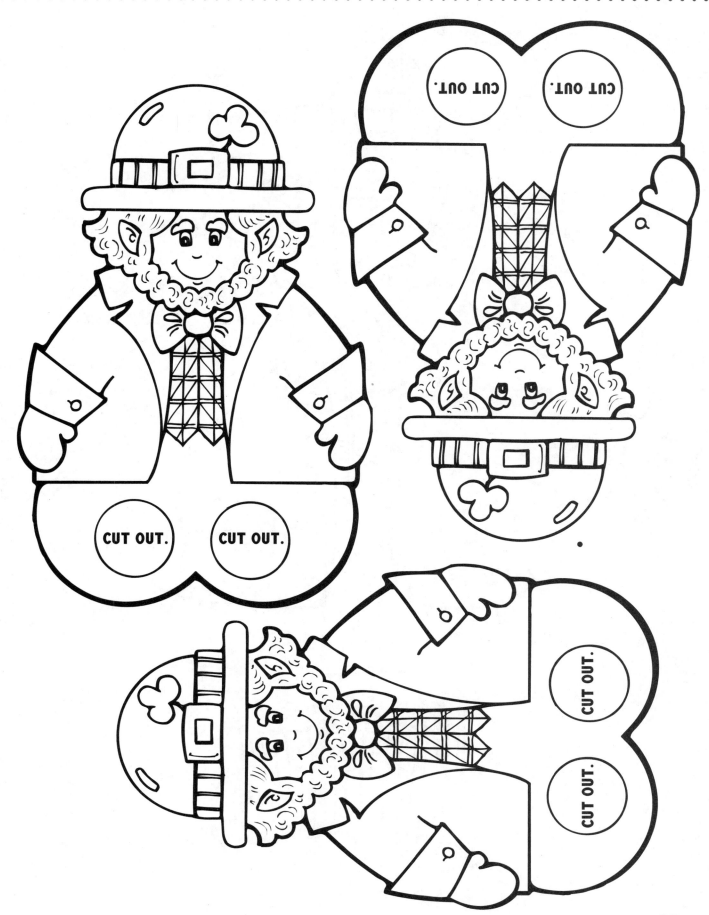

Lucky Leprechaun's

START

Pot-o'-Gold

FINISH

PLACE THIS SIDE ALONG FOLD.

JAPAN

The people of Japan live in a culture of ancient traditions and modern technologies. For students living in our world of instant news and easy-to-access Internet information, grasping the meaning of "culture" is essential for respecting the Japanese traditions started a millennia ago and still practiced today.

Modern Cultures, Ancient Festivals

One way for modern cultures to honor ancient traditions is through the celebration of festivals. The Japanese have many annual festivals. Some of the most notable spring festivals are Hina Matsuri (a doll festival) and Tango no Sekku (a kite festival).

Hina Matsuri On March 3rd, Japanese girls dress up in their finest kimonos and display treasured doll collections—dolls that have been passed down by their grandmothers and mothers. When visitors call on a family during this festival, they are served tea and sweet cakes and are invited to see the doll collection. If desired, bring elements of this festival to the classroom by inviting students (both boys and girls) to bring in their favorite dolls and action figures. Encourage volunteers to show the class their special item and tell why it is important to them.

Tango No Sekku On May 5th, Japanese boys attach fish kites to tall bamboo poles and fly the colorful kites in the family garden. One kite is usually flown for each boy in the family. On this day, you might invite your class to fly kites on the school playground. You'll find a pattern that students can use to make their own kites on page 56.

Suggested Activities

 ## MAP OF JAPAN

Help students learn about Japan's geography with this activity. First, distribute copies of the map of Japan (page 52). Then, using a globe or large world map, help students locate the islands that make up Japan. Explain that their map shows the location of a few of Japan's larger or more important cities. Review the list of city names on the page, then challenge students to label those cities on their map. They can use a world map, atlas, or Internet sources to help them complete the activity.

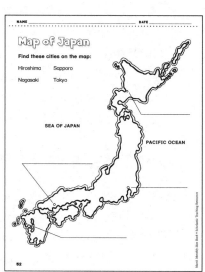

JAPANESE WORD FIND

Distribute copies of the word find on page 53. Explain to students that the word bank on the page contains words associated with Japanese culture. Review the words, then ask students to find and circle each one in the puzzle. After students complete the activity, work with them to define each word. You can provide dictionaries and other resources for students to use for this exercise. Write the words and their meanings on chart paper. Then, if desired, display the words on a class word wall. Finally, have students use some of the words from the puzzle in the writing assignment at the bottom of the page.

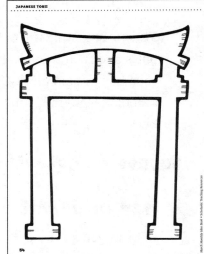

 ## TERRIFIC TORII

Torii (tor-ee-ee) are entryways that can be seen throughout Japan's varied landscapes. Since ancient times, torii have marked the entrances to religious shrines, like doorways between ordinary life and what is considered holy. According to tradition, it is considered good luck to walk under a torii. For this reason, some people who feel lucky in life fund the construction of a new torii as a way to express gratitude for their own good fortune.

Explain to students that there are many different types of torii, but they share a similar structure and purpose. Distribute photocopies of page 54 and discuss the architecture of the torii on that page. Invite students to color the torii an orange-red color. Then, in the space around the structure, have students write expressions of thanks or draw pictures depicting their own luck in life. To display, surround the frame of your class door with red bulletin board paper to create a giant torii. Then attach students' pages to the red torii where they can view and reflect on their good luck each time they pass through the door.

 ## PEARLS AND OYSTERS

Pearls are known in Japan as "the gift of kings." If possible, bring in a string of costume pearls and a few oysters from a local fish market. Have the oysters opened at the market so students will be able to see inside them. (Check for allergies before allowing students to handle the oysters.) As you show students the pearls and oysters, explain that often a grain of sand gets inside an oyster shell and becomes an irritant. Over time, the oyster coats the irritant to protect itself, and in the process, an iridescent pearl is formed from the layers. To learn more about pearls, work with students to find out how cultured pearls are made and how the pearl divers in Japan find pearls. Use a variety of resources, such as library books and the Internet to gather information.

After sharing your findings, use a pearl-and-oyster theme to reinforce students' knowledge about Japan. Photocopy and cut out a supply of the patterns on page 55 (there are two oyster shells for every pearl). Staple each pair of oyster shells together at the base. Then write a question about Japan on the top shell of each oyster and the answer on a pearl. If desired, use glitter crayons or glue to add decorative accents to the shells and pearls. To use, invite students to read and answer each question, matching each pearl to the corresponding oysters.

★ CARP FESTIVAL KITE

Invite students to make these fish-themed windsock kites to fly on a windy day. Give each student two photocopies of the fish kite pattern (page 56). Also provide students with blank sheets of paper, 3-feet lengths of paper streamers, glue, packing tape, and yarn. To make a kite, have students do the following:

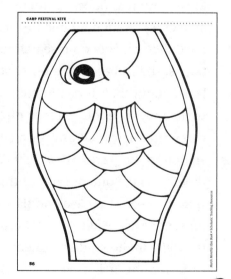

1. Color and cut out each fish pattern.

2. Form a tube with the cutouts by gluing the sides of the fish together (colored sides facing outward) and leaving the ends open.

3. Glue several paper streamers to the fish tail.

4. Use packing tape to attach each end of a length of yarn to the inside of the fish mouth, as shown.

5. Hold up the kite, or run with it, so the wind can flow through the opening of the kite. Or, tie the kite to a stationery object outdoors where it can capture the blowing wind.

★ FISH PUPPET

To make fish puppets for role-playing and dramatization, give each student a photocopy of the fish patterns (page 57) and a small paper bag. Then have students do the following:

1. Color the fish patterns and cut them out.

2. Glue the fish head to the bottom flap of the paper bag. Then glue the body to the front of the bag, as shown.

3. Glue on craft items, such as glitter, sequins, or ribbon, to embellish your fish.

4. Slip your hand into the bottom of the bag and use your fingers and thumb to make the fish's mouth open and close.

★ TRADITIONAL DRESS PUPPETS

Pair up students to write reports about topics related to Japanese culture (such as kimonos, kites, lanterns, bonsai gardens, fans, and abacuses). Assign a topic to each pair, and have the students do research using library books, the Internet, and other sources to learn about their topic. Encourage them to write a report about their findings. They can write their final drafts on copies of the stationery on pages 58 and 59. Then invite them to make one or both of the puppets (pages 60–61) to use as props for their presentations. After they color and cut out their puppets, invite students to embellish them with craft items—such as scraps of cloth, wrapping paper, wall paper samples, glitter, lace, and ribbon—to represent the traditional dress of the Japanese culture. Finally, have students glue a wide craft stick to the back of their puppets. Once students have completed their written reports and made their puppets, have them present their findings to the class.

★ JAPANESE POETRY WRITING

Invite students to write a special kind of poem called *haiku*. A haiku is a short, three-line verse about nature that is composed of a specific number of syllables in each line. The first and last lines each contain five syllables, and the middle line has seven syllables. In total, a haiku has 17 syllables.

Share the haiku below. As you read it aloud, have students count the number of syllables in it.

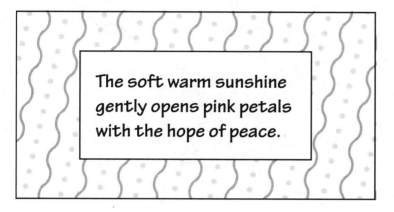

The soft warm sunshine
gently opens pink petals
with the hope of peace.

Next, invite students to write their own haikus. Following are some nature-related topics they might write about:

bird	honeybee	seed
butterfly	kite	springtime
cloud	lightning	tree
garden	pond	wind
grass	rain	

After students perfect their haikus, have them neatly record the poems in large print on a plain sheet of paper. Then have them mount their pages on pieces of decorative wrapping paper or wallpaper samples cut large enough to form a frame around their work. If desired, invite students to add illustrations to enhance their haikus.

Map of Japan

Find these cities on the map:

Hiroshima   Sapporo

Nagasaki   Tokyo

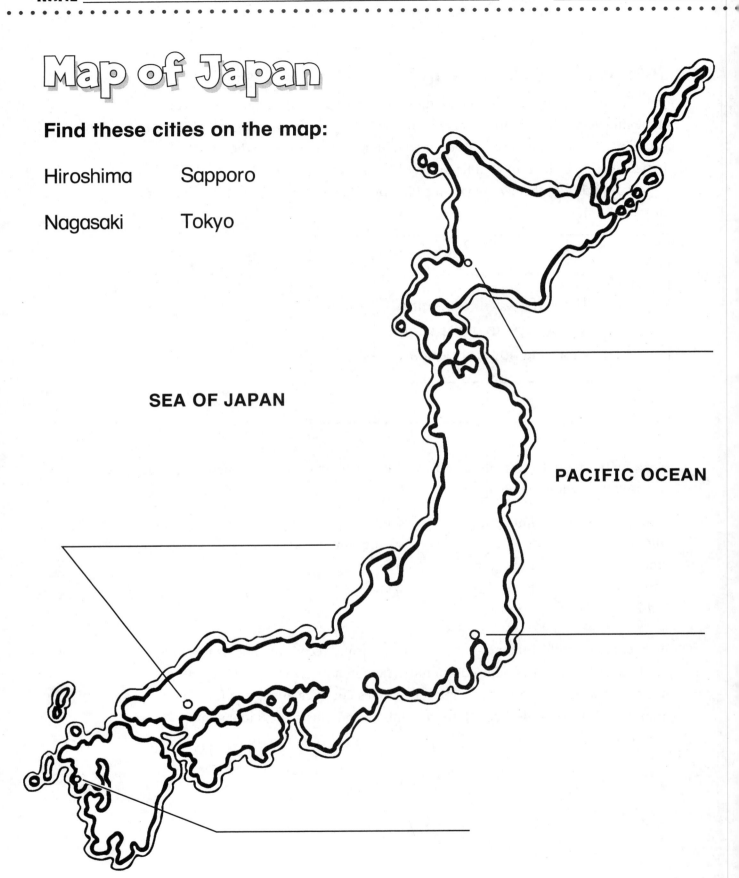

SEA OF JAPAN

PACIFIC OCEAN

Japanese Word Find

Find these words in the puzzle below:

ABACUS   FESTIVAL   HAIKU   JAPAN   KIMONO   KITE   KOI

LANTERN   LOTUS   OYSTER   SHRINE   TORII   TRADITION

```
A M S D F R E T G D F Q A S W D K R G B N M C D S J
A L C M A R Z H A C O V B G E N O Y S T E R K I G A
L E K I T E R T G J L D S H Z F I N H G A N I L I T
R X I S O A M R O C S R H G H E J U R N O L G T D U
P R M G R H Y J U D F R I G H S N J I O N H Y U G A
I E O E I C V G T D T R A D I T I O N M T S W A W O
L C N C I B G F D S O W B R T I R A E E O F R S E Y
X L O T U S T Y H G R Z A D C V I T R A X R G H J S
G O E K I C X M Z S I R C V J A P A N R E F G V B N
X U C V B G T A H A I K U N D L A N T E R N S E D F
A N S D F R C Y A S D C S F G D C V F G A U W U S T
A S X F E Y R X A R Y C H B H J K L O P M N G F D S
```

Using at least four words from the puzzle, write what you'd like to
learn about Japanese culture. If you need more space to write,
use the back of this page.

_____

_____

_____

_____

_____

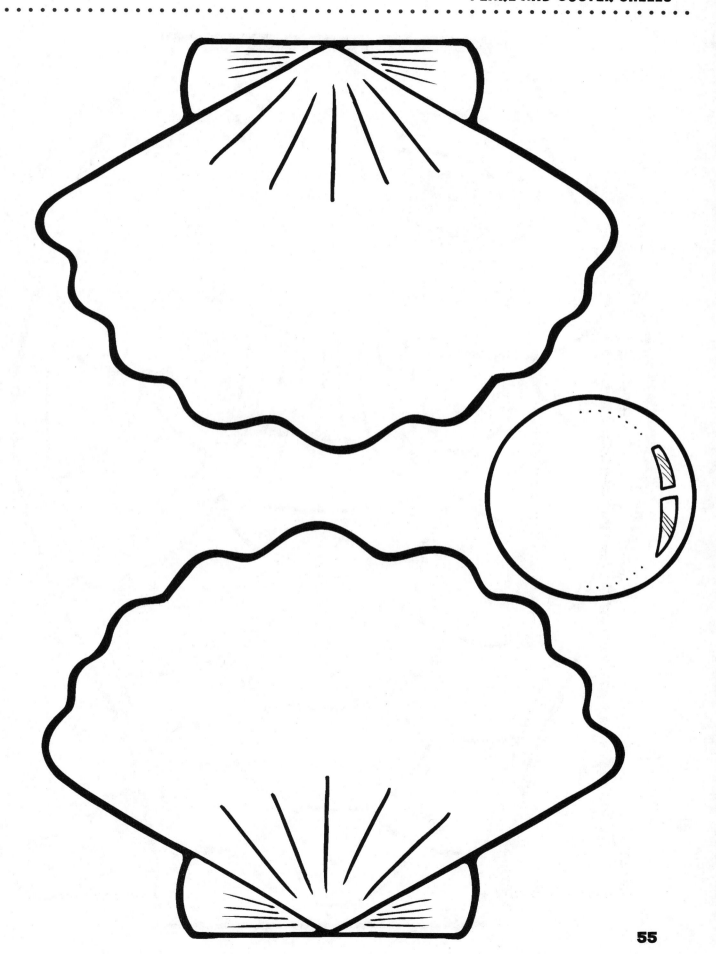

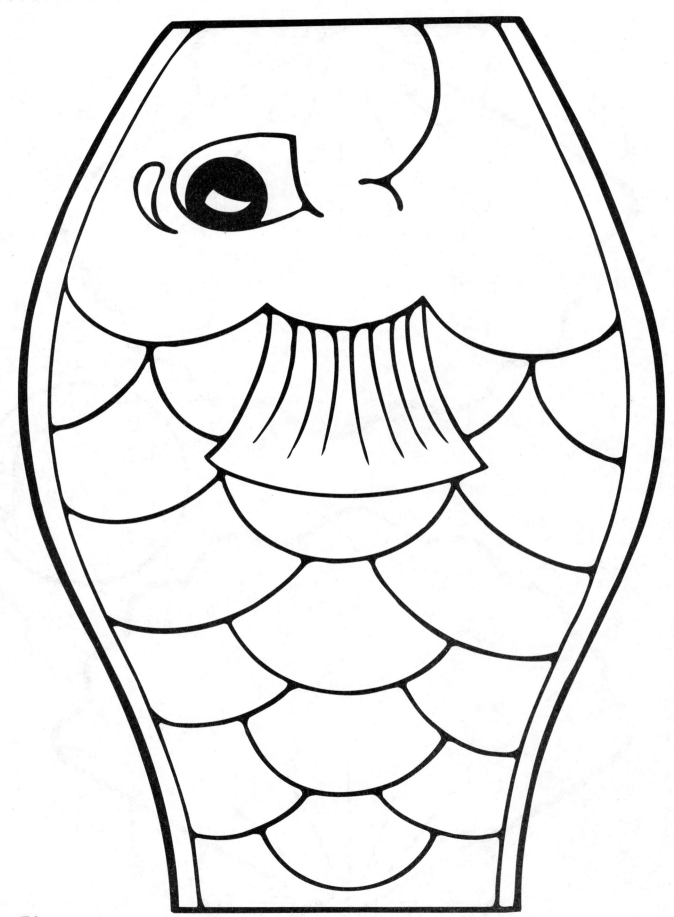

WOMEN IN HISTORY

Over the course of American history, women have been instrumental in shaping many aspects of our society from education, science, and transportation to commerce, labor, and national policies. After years of struggles, protests, and legislation, women in our country today enjoy many basic rights, such as the right to vote, own property, and obtain an education. But these issues are still points of contention in some cultures around the world where women may be denied the rights that women here cherish. In fact, women in some cultures are punished for attempting to exert their basic rights. As you discuss the role of women in American history, keep in mind the various cultures of your students and their families, showing sensitivity in the ways others might view or interpret specific issues.

International Women's Day

Each year on March 8, events are held throughout the world to celebrate the achievements of women across the globe. On this day—designed to honor and empower women—attention is also focused on the continued efforts to advance and achieve equality in all aspects for every woman. To make your students aware of this worldwide recognition of women, you might begin your studies of women in history on this day (or the school day immediately following it). For more information about International Women's Day, visit www.internationalwomensday.com/about.asp.

Suggested Activities

★ "EMPOWERED WOMEN" MEMORY GAME

Introduce students to some notable American women with this fun game. To begin, photocopy several sets of the name and fact cards on pages 65–68. You might copy each set on a different color of paper. Then, review the cards with students, matching each name to the corresponding fact. In advance, you might do some quick research to find more information about each woman to also share with students. If desired, include additional game cards for other historical women by labeling the blank name and fact cards on pages 69–70.

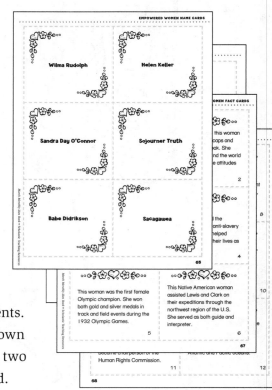

To play, give a set of cards to each small group of students. Ask students to shuffle their cards and arrange them facedown to form a grid. Then have students take turns flipping over two cards at a time to try to find a matching name and fact card.

If they find a match, students keep the cards. If not, they return the cards facedown to the grid. The game ends when all of the matches have been found. The student with the most matches is the winner. Below are the corresponding name and fact card pairs.

Name Card	Fact Card	Name Card	Fact Card
Wilma Rudolph	1	Susan B. Anthony	7
Helen Keller	2	Elizabeth Cady Stanton	8
Sandra Day O'Connor	3	Clara Barton	9
Sojourner Truth	4	Harriet Tubman	10
Babe Didrikson	5	Eleanor Roosevelt	11
Sacagawea	6	Amelia Earhart	12

★ LEGENDARY-LADIES GUESSING GAME

Play this game with students to reinforce their knowledge of several legendary ladies who have contributed to American history. To prepare, photocopy and color several sets of pages 71–76, then mount each picture on a sheet of construction paper. Divide the class into small groups (six or fewer students per group) and give each group a set of pictures and a clothespin. To play, a group will secretly choose a picture and clip it to the back of the shirt of one of their group members. That student will turn his or her back to the group and then ask "yes" and "no" questions to try to determine the identity of the pictured lady. For example, the student might ask, "Is the lady an athlete?" or "Did she live during the Civil War?" Encourage the student to try to guess the identity using as few clues as possible. Once that student correctly guesses the person, invite another student to take the role of guesser. Continue the game until every student in the group has had a turn to ask questions and identity a mystery lady.

FAMOUS WOMEN WORD FIND

Use the word find on page 77 to introduce students to more names of historical women. Explain that they will search the puzzle to find the last names of the women, but the first names are also provided. Then read aloud the names in the word bank on the page. If desired, do a little advance research so you can provide a few facts or bits of interesting information about each woman as you introduce her name.

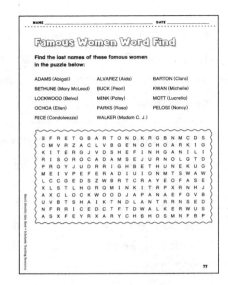

 ## "REMARKABLE WOMAN" REPORT

Invite students to research and write about a history-making woman whom they find interesting or inspiring. To begin, make a list of women's names from which students can choose their subject. List the names shown on the "Empowered Women" name cards (pages 65–66), in the word bank from "Famous Women Word Find" (page 77), and additional names that students brainstorm as a class. Then distribute photocopies of page 78 to students. Have them choose a woman to research and then use library books, the Internet, and other sources to gather information about their subject and to complete their report. Afterward, invite each student to share his or her report with the class. Finally, collect the reports and bind them behind a photocopy of the book cover on page 79. Write your class name on the author line, invite a few volunteers to color the cover, then place the book in your class library for students to enjoy.

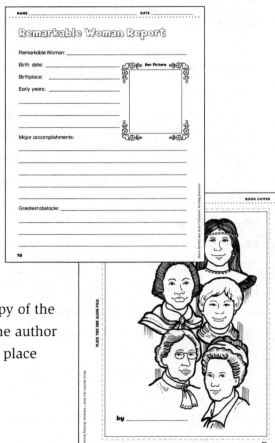

Wilma Rudolph

Helen Keller

Sandra Day O'Connor

Sojourner Truth

Babe Didrikson

Sacagawea

Susan B. Anthony

Elizabeth Cady Stanton

Clara Barton

Harriet Tubman

Eleanor Roosevelt

Amelia Earhart

This talented Olympic athlete was one of 19 children. She overcame childhood paralysis to win three gold medals in the 1960 Olympic Games.

1

Both deaf and blind, this woman overcame her handicaps and taught herself to speak. She gave speeches around the world in an effort to change attitudes toward the disabled.

2

This woman was named the first female Supreme Court Justice of the United States. She served on the court for 24 years before resigning in 2006.

3

This woman traveled the country speaking at anti-slavery meetings. She also helped former slaves build their lives as free people.

4

This woman was the first female Olympic champion. She won both gold and silver medals in track and field events during the 1932 Olympic Games.

5

This Native American woman assisted Lewis and Clark on their expeditions through the northwest region of the U.S. She served as both guide and interpreter.

6

A determined crusader for women's right to vote, this woman was once arrested for attempting to vote. One version of the dollar coin features her image.

7

This woman organized the first Women's Rights Convention. She encouraged women to fight for their rights to own property, obtain an education, vote, and hold political office.

8

This brave woman delivered medical supplies to the battlefields of the American Civil War. She later organized the American Red Cross.

9

Before the American Civil War, this woman risked her own freedom to travel into slave territories in an effort to lead other escaped slaves to freedom.

10

After her husband's death, this influential First Lady was appointed the U.S. representative to the United Nations. She later became chairperson of the Human Rights Commission.

11

This woman was the first female to fly solo across the Atlantic Ocean. She was also the first person to fly across both the Atlantic and Pacific oceans.

12

March Monthly Idea Book © Scholastic Teaching Resources

March Monthly Idea Book © Scholastic Teaching Resources

March Monthly Idea Book © Scholastic Teaching Resources

Famous Women Word Find

Find the last names of these famous women in the puzzle below:

ADAMS (Abigail)   ALVAREZ (Aida)   BARTON (Clara)

BETHUNE (Mary McLeod)   BUCK (Pearl)   KWAN (Michelle)

LOCKWOOD (Belva)   MINK (Patsy)   MOTT (Lucretia)

OCHOA (Ellen)   PARKS (Rosa)   PELOSI (Nancy)

RICE (Condoleezza)   WALKER (Madam C. J.)

```
S F R E T G B A R T O N D K R G B N M C D S
C M V R Z A C L V B G E N O C H O A R K I G
K I T E R G J V D S H E F I N H G A N I L I
R I S O R O C A D A M S E J U R N O L G T D
P R G Y J U D R R I G H B E T H U N E K U G
M E I V P E F E R A D I U I O N M T S W A W
L C C G E D S Z W B R T C R A Y E O F A S E
X L S T L H G R Q M I N K I T R P X R N H J
A X C L O C K W O O D J A P A N A E F G V B
U V B T S H A I K T N D L A N T R R N S E D
N F R R I C E D C T F T D W A L K E R W U S
A S X F E Y R X A R Y C H B H O S M N F B P
```

Remarkable Woman Report

Remarkable Woman: _____

Birth date: _____

Birthplace: _____

Early years: _____

_____

_____

_____

Her Picture

Major accomplishments:

_____

_____

_____

_____

_____

Greatest obstacle: _____

_____

_____

_____

_____

March Monthly Idea Book © Scholastic Teaching Resources

Remarkable
Women

PLACE THIS SIDE ALONG FOLD.

by _____

MARVELOUS MUSIC!

From an early age, most children are exposed to music in a variety of forms, from parents singing lullabies to recordings of soothing symphonies to lively performances of childhood tunes such as the "Alphabet Song" and "Old McDonald." As an introduction to this unit, ask students to share about the many ways music fits into their daily activities. Then use the cross-curricular ideas presented here to help students explore and develop an appreciation for different aspects of music.

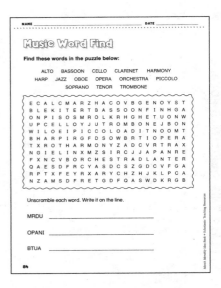

Suggested Activities

 ## MUSIC WORD FIND

Use the word find on page 84 to help students become familiar with music-related vocabulary. After students complete the activity, tell them that the word scramble at the bottom features three additional words for instruments that are not in the word find. Have them unscramble those words, then review each word from the page. Finally, list the words on chart paper and work with students to define each one.

 ## INSTRUMENT MATCH

Challenge students to match instruments to their names with this center activity. First, display photos of different kinds of instruments. Talk with students about the characteristics of each instrument, such as the mouthpiece, reed, and keys on a clarinet. Then photocopy, color, cut apart, and laminate the picture and word cards on pages 85–86. Place the cards in a learning center for student use. The correct picture and word card pairs are: 1–violin, 2–guitar, 3–trumpet, 4–flute, 5–clarinet, 6–French horn, 7–drum, and 8–cymbals.

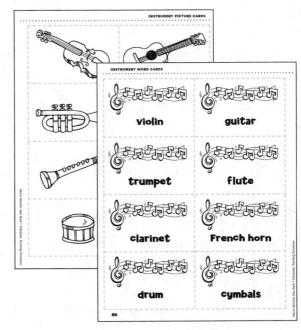

MUSICAL WORD WALL

Create a word wall filled with music-related words to reinforce students' vocabulary. Simply photocopy a supply of the music notes on page 87. (If desired, copy them in a variety of colors.) Then cut out the notes and label them with words from the word find (page 84) and instrument cards (page 86), as well as other words that connect to music and musical concepts. To display, attach the notes in a random arrangement on your word wall, or create one or more music staffs on which to position the notes. You can create a music staff by making five parallel lines along the wall, spacing them evenly apart, as shown.

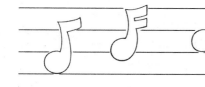

 ## MARCHING BAND HAT

Students can make their own marching band hats to add fanfare and flare to a class parade. First, photocopy the hat patterns on pages 88–89 and distribute to students along with sentence strips (for headbands). Then have students do the following to make their hats:

1. Color and cut out the feather and hat patterns.

2. Glue the feather to the front of the hat, as shown.

3. Fold the bill of the hat up along the dashed line.

4. Glue the hat to the middle of the sentence strip.

5. With the help of a partner, fit the sentence strip around their head and staple the ends together. Then trim off any excess.

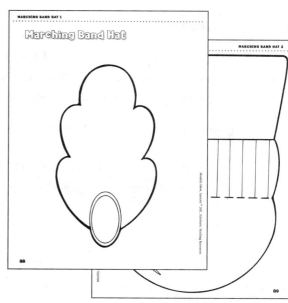

Invite students to don their hats and play rhythm instruments as they parade around the classroom or school. (Or students might use the instruments they make in "Quick-and-Easy Instruments" on page 82.)

QUICK-AND-EASY INSTRUMENTS

Explain to students that instruments vibrate to make music. Each instrument vibrates in its own way to make sound. For instance, guitar strings vibrate as they are strummed and a drum top vibrates when it is struck. When a musician plays a clarinet, the reed vibrates, and a tuba vibrates when the player blows into the mouthpiece. Invite students to make the instruments below, then challenge them to explore how their instruments vibrate to make music.

Drum

Decorate an empty coffee canister. Then put on the lid to complete the drum. Use two craft sticks as drumsticks to play the instrument.

Maracas

Place a handful of dried beans into two recyclable plastic containers that have lids (such as small butter tubs). Snap on the lids, then shake the containers to create a rhythmic sound.

Rhythm Blocks

Cover two small blocks of wood with sandpaper. Rub the blocks together to make a swish-swish sound.

Kazoo

Wrap a piece of wax paper around a plastic fine-toothed comb. To play, place the comb—teeth up—against the lips and hum. The teeth and paper will vibrate, creating a kazoo-like sound.

Spoons

Hold a pair of plastic or metal spoons back-to-back loosely between the fingers. Tap the spoons against the knee to create a clickety-click sound. (The secret is to hold the spoons lightly.)

Guitar

Stretch three rubber bands around a small shoe box. Space them evenly apart. Then strum the rubber bands with the fingers to play the guitar.

★ TUBA-TOP TALES

Have students compose tales about their own musical experiences. They might write about playing instruments, attending a concert, or marching to music in a parade. Or, they might make up an imaginary story related to music. As students write, encourage them to incorporate vocabulary words and concepts that they have learned in their study of music. Distribute photocopies of the tuba patterns on pages 90–91 for students to use for their final copies. Ask them to cut out the patterns, color the bear, and glue the tuba bell to the top of the bear's instrument. Then have them write their text on the bell. When finished, invite volunteers to share their written work with the class. Afterward, display students' work on a bulletin board.

As a variation, you might have students write about their achievements as a way to "blow their own horns." To display, post students' work on a display titled, "Tootin' Our Own Horns!"

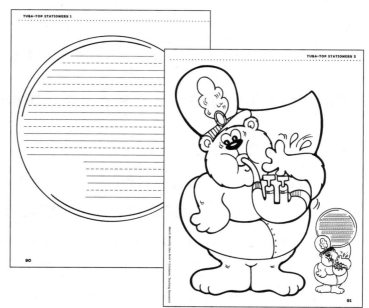

★ MUSICAL MESSAGES

Tell students that in 1933, the first singing telegram was delivered in New York City. Explain that a singing telegram is a message set to a tune. After sharing this bit of trivia, invite students to create their own singing telegrams. To begin, ask them to decide what their message will be and to whom they want to send it (perhaps to the principal, members of the school staff, or students in another class). Then have students decide on a tune to use for their message—familiar childhood songs, such as "Twinkle, Twinkle, Little Star" and "The Itsy Bitsy Spider" work well. When students are ready to write their final drafts, distribute copies of the stationery on page 92. After completing their messages, allow time in class for students to practice singing the lyrics before they set out to deliver them to the recipients.

Music Word Find

Find these words in the puzzle below:

ALTO   BASSOON   CELLO   CLARINET   HARMONY

HARP   JAZZ   OBOE   OPERA   ORCHESTRA   PICCOLO

SOPRANO   TENOR ,   TROMBONE

```
E C A L C M A R Z H A C O V B G E N O Y S T
B L E K I T E R T B A S S O O N F I N H G A
O N P I S O S M R O L K R H G H E T U O N W
U P C E L L O Y J U T R O M B O N E J B O N
W I L O E I P I C C O L O A D I T N O O M T
B H A R P I R G F D S O W B R T I O P E R A
T X R O T H A R M O N Y Z A D C V R T R A X
N G I E L I N X M Z S I R C J J A P A N R E
F X N C V B O R C H E S T R A D L A N T E R
Q A E S D F R C Y A S D C S Z G D C V F G A
R P T X F E Y R X A R Y C H Z H J K L P C A
N Z A M S D F R E T G D F Q A S W D K R G B
```

Unscramble each word. Write it on the line.

MRDU _____

OPANI _____

BTUA _____

1

2

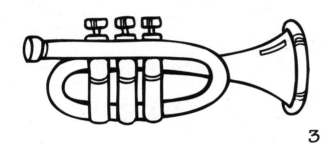

3

4

5

6

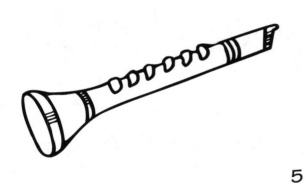

7

8

violin

guitar

trumpet

flute

clarinet

French horn

drum

cymbals

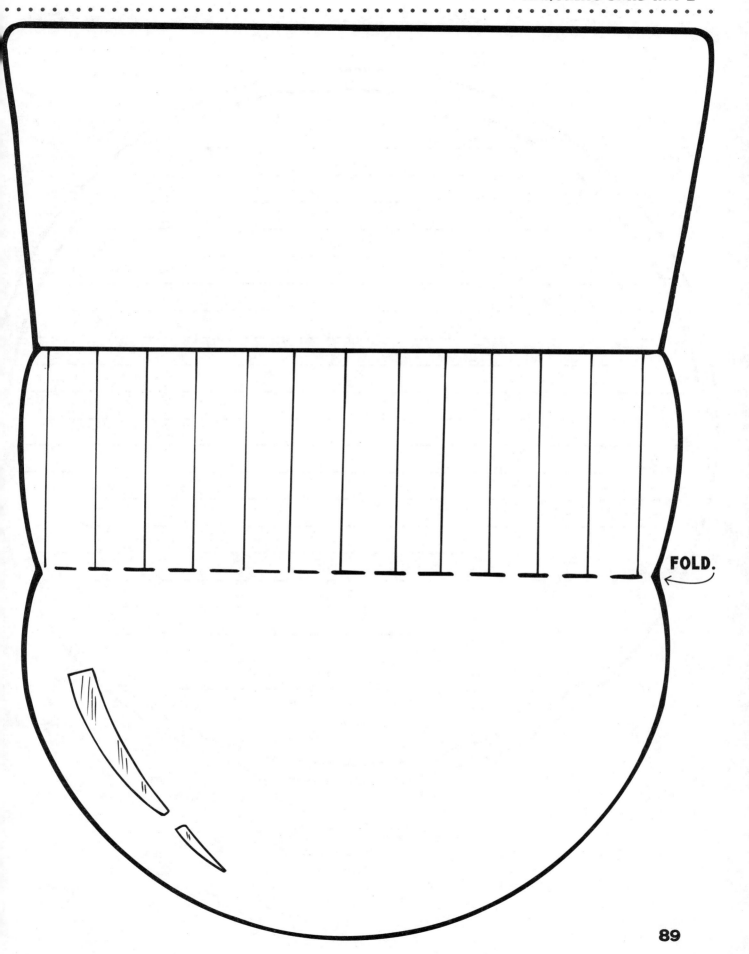

FOLD.

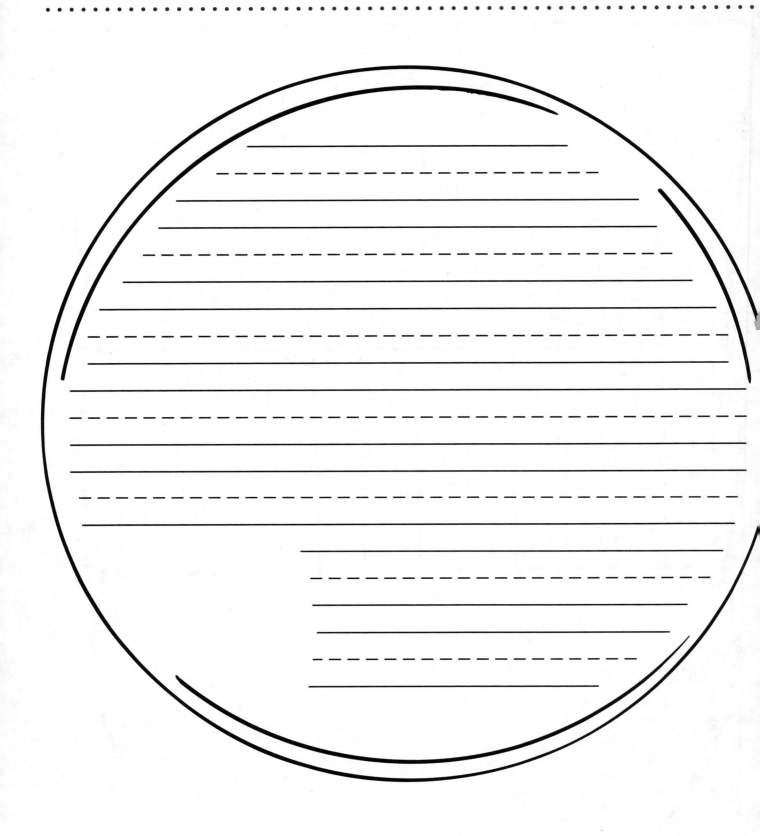

SPRING WEATHER

As long as mankind has been recording history, people have been recording the weather. Those records and man's ingenuity have given us trusted strategies for predicting and coping with weather. Many of those strategies have been passed down through written and oral traditions. We've become familiar with lore such as, "March comes in like a lion and goes out like a lamb." To inform decisions about planting crops and gathering harvests, most every culture has developed sophisticated ways of recording and learning about factors that impact the weather. The result has been the development of instruments for gathering information, forecasting, and warning people about changes in weather and climate change.

Suggested Activities

 ## SPRINGTIME BINGO

Reinforce spring-related vocabulary words with a game of Bingo! To prepare, make several photocopies of the game board on page 99. On each page, fill in the vocabulary words you want students to practice, using the same words but in a different arrangement on each game board. (You might use words from the word-find word bank on page 100, as well as other words related to spring weather or new growth associated with the season.) Write each word on a plain index card. Copy the programmed game boards, making enough for each student in a group (or the whole class) to have one, then laminate. To use, supply players with Bingo chips or dried beans to use as markers, then have a caller choose one word card at a time to read to players. When players find that word on their game board, they cover it with a marker. Continue play until players have covered all of the words on their game boards. At that time, all the players call out "Bingo!" together.

SPRING WEATHER WORD FIND

Distribute copies of the word find (page 100) to students and review the weather words listed on the page. After they complete the activity, have students use words from the puzzle to write about springtime weather.

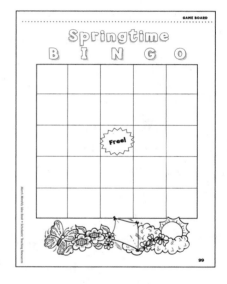

SPRING QUOTE DECODER

Challenge students to decode a hidden quote related to March weather. Give students photocopies of page 101 and have them color in each odd-numbered block in the grid. When finished, ask them to write the remaining letters on the lines at the bottom of the page to reveal the common quote. After students have decoded the quote, read it aloud with them, then discuss its meaning.

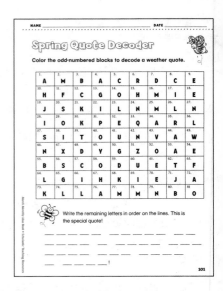

 WEATHER WHEEL

Review with students the different kinds of spring weather they might experience. Explain that during spring, the cold weather of winter is ending and the warmer weather leading to summer is arriving—this transition often causes some unusual and unpredictable weather for this season. Then invite students to make a weather wheel that they can use to identify the daily weather, or even weather changes throughout the day! To make, distribute tagboard photocopies of pages 102–103 and brass fasteners to students and have them do the following.

1. Color and cut out each pattern. Write their name on the line.

2. Carefully cut out the shape on the title wheel.

3. Stack the wheels with the title wheel on top. Use a brass fastener to attach the wheels to each other.

4. Turn the back wheel until the desired weather condition appears in the opening of the front wheel.

 TODAY'S WEATHER REPORT

Your young weather forecasters can fill out the weather report (page 104) to record local weather conditions and more for the day. After distributing photocopies of the page, have students check the daily paper, Internet, or weather broadcast to gather the information they need to complete the report. When

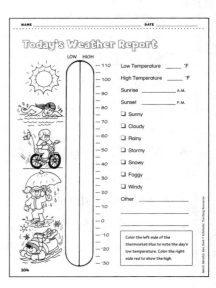

completed, invite students to share, compare, and discuss their findings. As a follow-up, you might collect the daily reports, then use them for graphing or other math activities.

WEATHER-RELATED CRAFTS

Invite students to make these weather-inspired crafts to use as props or meteorology "instruments" as they explore the often-windy conditions of spring.

Weather Forecaster Visor

To liven up students' forecasts, make tagboard photocopies of the visor pattern (page 105) for them to color and cut out. Then ask them to write their name on the line, and punch a hole at each end of the visor, where indicated. Finally, have students add a length of elasticized string to fit the visor to their head. Invite students to wear their visors when they fill out their weather reports (page 104) or do other weather-related activities.

Wind-Detector Pinwheel

Students can use these pinwheels outdoors on a windy day. Provide each student with a photocopy of the pinwheel pattern (page 106), a straight pin, and an unsharpened pencil with a rubber eraser at one end. Have students do the following to make their pinwheel (supervise students closely when working with the straight pins):

1. Color and cut out the pinwheel pattern.

2. Cut along the dashed line at each corner of the pattern, stopping where indicated. Using the dots as a guide, bring each corner to the center dot, overlapping the tips of the corners. You might dab a bit of glue between the tips to help hold them in place. (Do not make creases in the pinwheel.)

3. To make a handle, poke a straight pin through the center of the pinwheel and into the pencil eraser.

4. Now, blow your pinwheel! If it does not move freely, make the pinhole slightly larger until the pinwheel spins easily when air blows it.

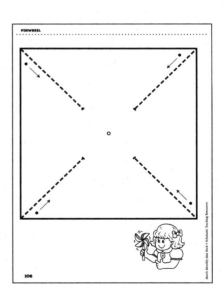

Paper-Bag Windsock

Students can use this easy-to-make windsock to check the direction of the wind. Provide small paper bags, 18-inch lengths of crepe-paper streamers in a variety of colors, glue, a hole-punch, and yarn. Then have students do the following to make a windsock:

1. Cut out the bottom of the bag. Color and decorate the bag any way they desire.

2. Glue three or four 18-inch streamers to one end of the bag.

3. Punch four holes near the opposite end of the bag, as shown.

4. Cut four 6-inch lengths of yarn. Tie each one to a hole. Then tie the other ends of the of yarn together, attaching them to a longer length of yarn, as shown.

 ## OVER-THE-RAINBOW MOBILE

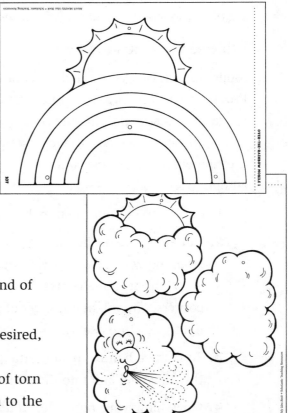

Whether your class is studying weather or rainbows, these mobiles are easy to make and display. Give each student a photocopy of the mobile patterns (pages 107–108), two 1-foot lengths of yarn, and scissors. Also provide glue, clear tape, and an assortment of craft items, such as glitter, cotton balls, iridescent tinsel icicles (as used on Christmas trees), and tissue-paper scraps in the colors of the rainbow. Then have students do the following to make their mobile:

1. Cut out the rainbow and cloud patterns.

2. On the back of each cutout, write about the kind of weather represented on the front.

3. Color or decorate the front of each cutout. If desired, use craft items to add texture and interest. For example, glue glitter to the sun, attach pieces of torn tissue to the bands of the rainbow, glue cotton to the clouds, and tape a few icicles to the plain cloud to represent falling rain.

4. Punch holes in the rainbow and clouds where indicated.

5. Cut one of the 1-foot lengths of yarn into three pieces of varying lengths. Tie a length of yarn to the hole in each cloud. Tie the other end to a hole at the bottom of the rainbow, as shown.

6. To make a hanger, tie the other 1-foot length of yarn to the top of the rainbow.

★ SPRING DRAMATIZATION PROPS

Most folks associate lions and lambs with the changeable weather in March—such as the blustery beginning and balmy end of the month. To make puppets for pretend play and dramatizations, invite students to make these puppets.

Animal Finger Puppets

Distribute copies of the lion and lamb finger puppet patterns on page 109. Have students color and cut out the patterns. Then help them cut out the holes on the front of each animal puppet, as needed. To use, students poke their fingers through the holes in a puppet and wiggle them around to serve as legs for the animal.

Paper-Plate Puppets

Provide students with the animal puppet patterns on pages 110–111, 9-inch paper plates, wide craft sticks, scissors, glue, and craft items, such as yellow yarn and cotton balls. Then have students follow these directions to make their puppets:

1. Color and cut out each animal pattern.

2. Glue each animal cutout to a paper plate.

3. For the lion's mane, fringe the rim of the plate around the animal's face. Or, glue on short lengths of yarn.

4. For the lamb, glue cotton balls to the top of the animal's head to create a fluffy patch of wool.

5. Glue a craft stick to the back of each puppet.

RAINY-DAY READING LOG

Give each student a photocopy of the reading log on page 112. Explain that students will select and read books from each category shown on the umbrella. If desired, gather a collection of books representing the different categories to put in your class library. Or, help students find books in the school library that fall under each category. After students read a book, have them record its title and author in the section of the umbrella that corresponds to the category the book belongs to. Periodically, invite students to share their reading log with the class and to make reading recommendations.

 ## RAINBOW STORY STARTERS

Invite students to write colorful stories to wrap up their studies of spring weather. First, explain that sometimes a rainbow can be seen in the sky after a spring rain. The arced bands of a rainbow are represented by seven colors as follows, starting with the outer band and ending with the inner band: red, orange, yellow, green, blue, indigo, and violet. (Often indigo and violet are combined into one color when teaching young children about the rainbow.) Then challenge students to write creative, imaginative stories in which they use each of the rainbow colors. Here are some ideas for story starters:

- ■ *After tapping his cane on it twice, he lifted the . . .*

- ■ *At the back of the cave was a twisted . . .*

- ■ *Boing! If that ball bounced any higher it would . . .*

- ■ *Lumbering down the street was the biggest . . .*

- ■ *Only one more wish was left, so I . . .*

- ■ *The young girl ran from her garden when she spotted a . . .*

- ■ *When the elf stopped hopping, I knew. . .*

After students write their final drafts, distribute photocopies of the book cover on page 113. Have them color the cover, add a title and author line, then staple to their stories to create a book.

Springtime
BINGO

Free!

Spring Weather Word Find

Find these words in the puzzle below:

CLOUDY   COOL   FAIR   HOT   MILD

RAINY   SHOWERS   STORMY   SUNNY

TEMPERATURE   THUNDER   WINDY

```
E C A L C S A R Z H A C O V B W I N D Y S T
B L E K I P E R T B A C S O O S F I D H G A
O F P I S G S M R O L G U N S H V N J O N W
U A C S T O R M Y U T R O T B O N E W B O N
W I L O E L P U C O O L S H D W T N O O M T
B R A K P T E M P E R A T U R E I O P E R A
T X C O T S L B Y J U T R N M R A I N Y A X
N G L E L I N R M H O T U D J S A P A N R E
F X O C V B O M C H E S T E A D L A M T E R
Q S U L B F B I O Z S O M R E G D C V F G A
R P D X F E Y L X A R Y C H Z H J K L P C A
N Z Y M S R F D E T G D F Q A S U N N Y G B
```

Using six of the words from the puzzle, write about springtime weather. If you need more space to write, use the back of this page.

_____

_____

_____

_____

Spring Quote Decoder

Color the odd-numbered blocks to decode a weather quote.

1. A	2. M	3. B	4. A	5. C	6. R	7. D	8. C	9. E
10. H	11. F	12. C	13. G	14. O	15. H	16. M	17. I	18. E
19. J	20. S	21. K	22. I	23. L	24. N	25. M	26. L	27. N
28. I	29. O	30. K	31. P	32. E	33. Q	34. A	35. R	36. L
37. S	38. I	39. T	40. O	41. U	42. N	43. V	44. A	45. W
46. N	47. X	48. D	49. Y	50. G	51. Z	52. O	53. A	54. E
55. B	56. S	57. C	58. O	59. D	60. U	61. E	62. T	63. F
64. L	65. G	66. I	67. H	68. K	69. I	70. E	71. J	72. A
73. K	74. L	75. L	76. A	77. M	78. M	79. N	80. B	81. O

Write the remaining letters in order on the lines. This is the special quote!

___ ___ ___ ___ ___   ___ ___ ___ ___ ___   ___ ___

___ ___ ___ ___   ___ ___ ___ ___ ___   ___ ___ ___

___ ___ ___ ___ ___   ___ ___ ___ ___

___ ___ ___ ___ ___!

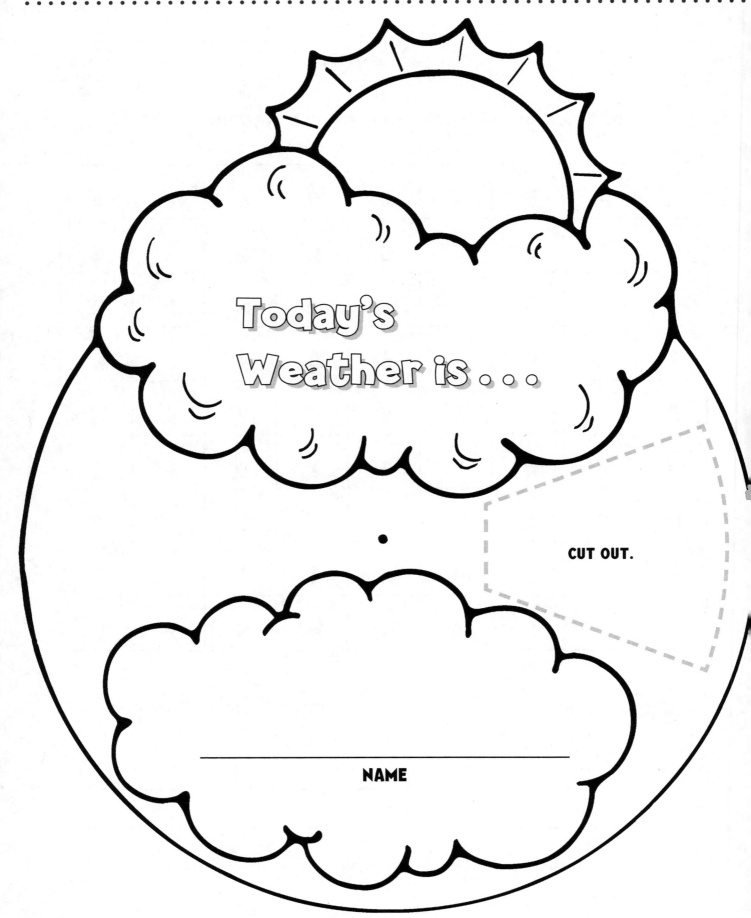

Today's
Weather is . . .

CUT OUT.

_____
NAME

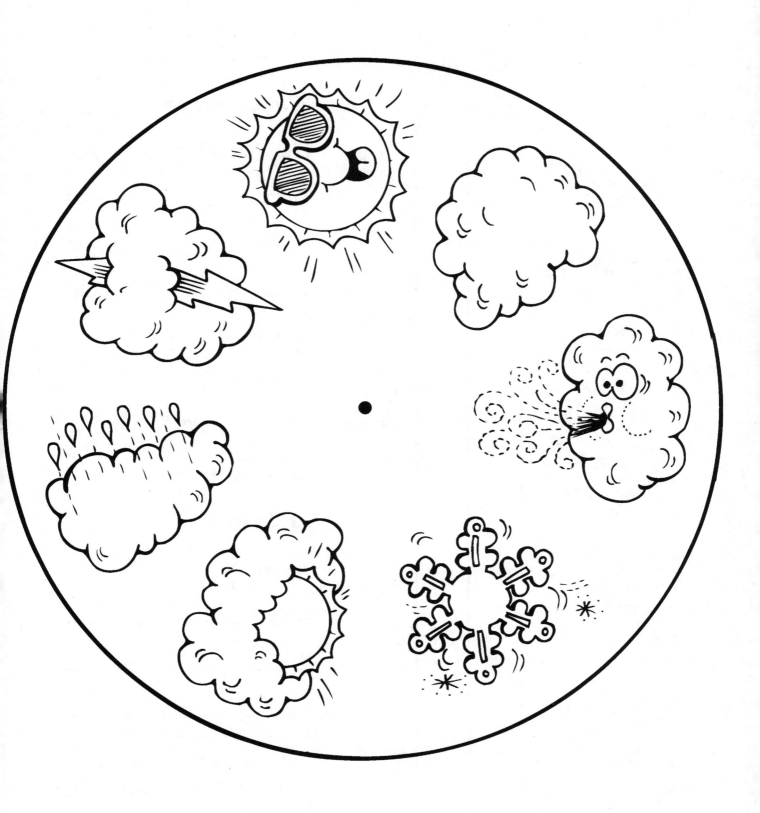

Today's Weather Report

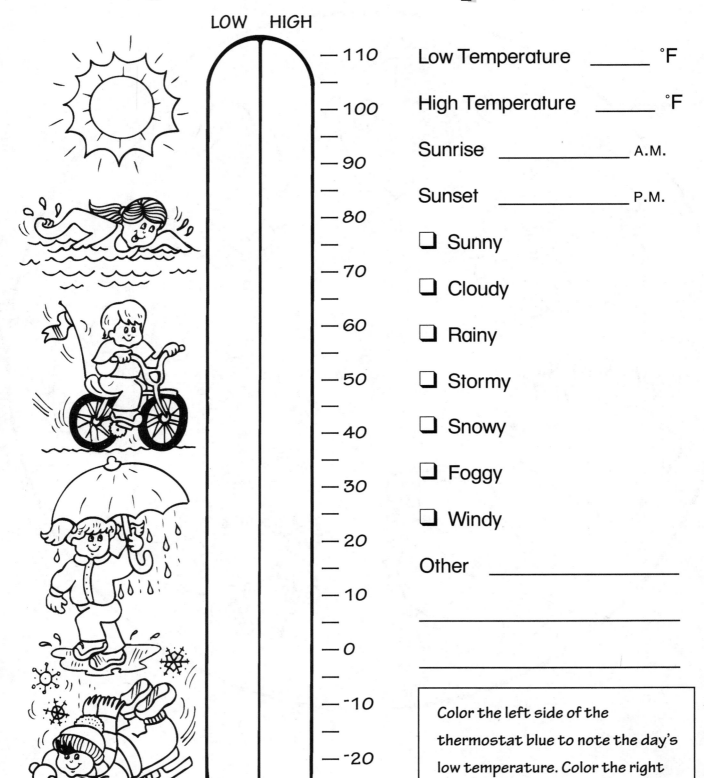

LOW   HIGH

— 110
—
— 100
—
— 90
—
— 80
—
— 70
—
— 60
—
— 50
—
— 40
—
— 30
—
— 20
—
— 10
—
— 0
—
— -10
—
— -20
—
— -30

Low Temperature _____ °F

High Temperature _____ °F

Sunrise _____ A.M.

Sunset _____ P.M.

❏ Sunny

❏ Cloudy

❏ Rainy

❏ Stormy

❏ Snowy

❏ Foggy

❏ Windy

Other _____

_____

_____

Color the left side of the thermostat blue to note the day's low temperature. Color the right side red to show the high.

NAME

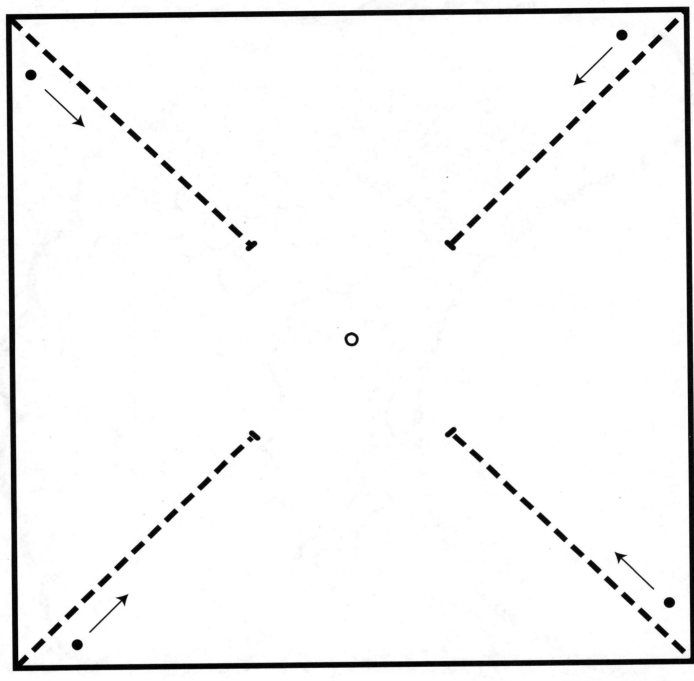

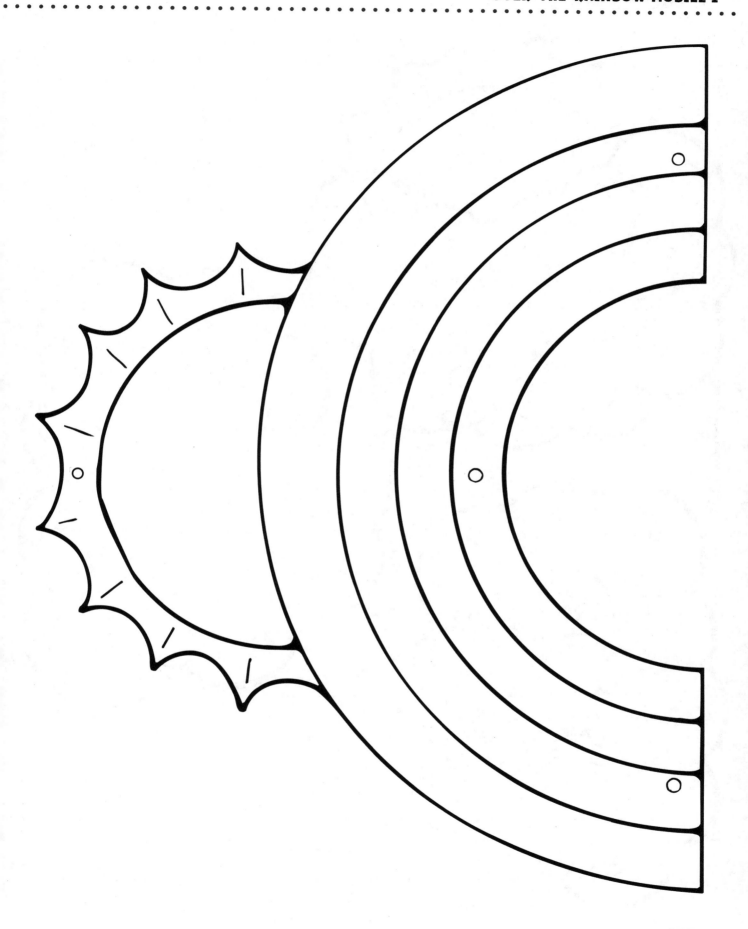

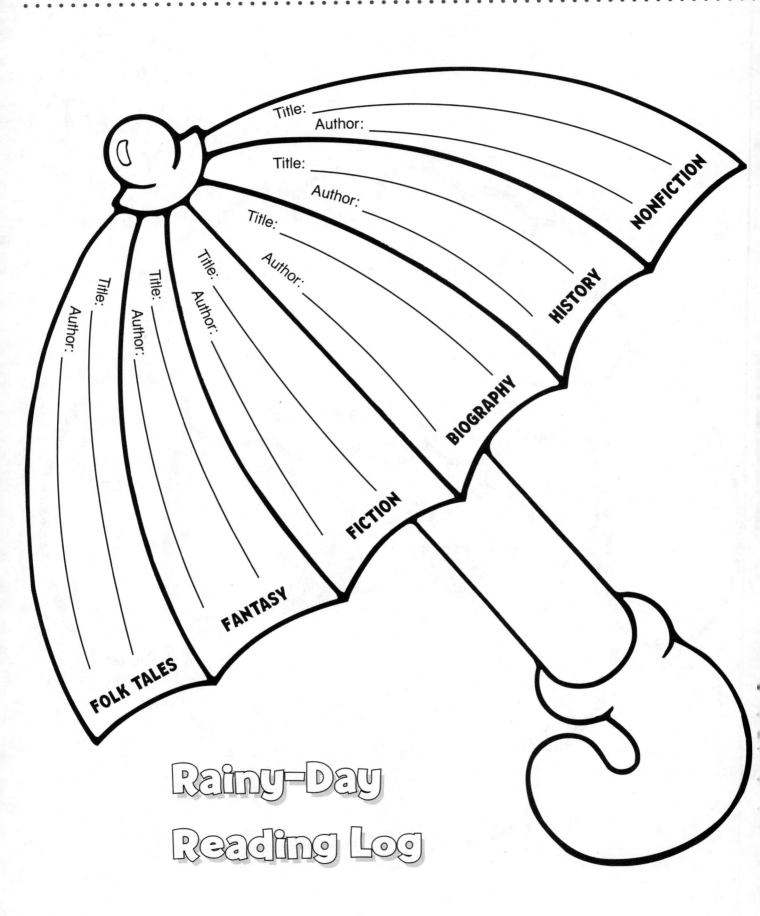

Title: _____
Author: _____

Title: _____
Author: _____

Title: _____
Author: _____

Title: _____
Author: _____

Title: _____
Author: _____

Title: _____
Author: _____

NONFICTION

HISTORY

BIOGRAPHY

FICTION

FANTASY

FOLK TALES

Rainy-Day
Reading Log

DOWN ON THE FARM

The development of farms meant that, instead of following herds of animals and searching for game, people were able to eat the meat of animals they could tend and contain in fences. Instead of hunting for roots and gathering berries, people could plant and harvest crops to use for food. As you discuss farming with students, talk about the traditional and changing role of farms in our society and the contributions they make to our food supply.

Suggested Activities

FARM-TIME RHYTHM AND RHYME

Begin your farm studies with a musical introduction. Invite students to name songs or chants about farm animals that they are familiar with. Most likely, they will respond with childhood favorites, such as "Old McDonald," "This Little Piggy," and "Mary Had a Little Lamb." As students name a song or chant, invite a volunteer to lead the class in singing or reciting it. Afterward, call on students to share about ways the lyrics relate to a farm or farm life. Also, ask them to share other information they know about farms from sources other than songs or chants, such as books, television, or even firsthand experience.

FARM-FRIENDLY FIELD TRIPS

Contact your local Farm Bureau, 4-H Club, or Future Farmers of America regarding a class trip to a farm. Or, if you live in a more urban setting, consider planning a trip to a petting zoo that houses farm animals. If arranging transportation to a farm or petting zoo is problematic, you might invite a local farmer or petting zoo representative to visit your classroom. Before the event, ask parent volunteers to help prepare for the visit and be available to take pictures of any animals your visitor might bring in. Then, after the event, have students write and draw about what they learned and their observations. Finally, prepare a display in the classroom to showcase the photos, students' work, and other highlights about the experience.

FARM WORD FINDS

Use this activity to build student's farm-related vocabulary. To begin, work with the class to brainstorm words associated with farms, such as different kinds of farm animals (parents and babies), farm buildings, and crops grown on a farm. Record student responses on chart paper. Then post the list in an easily accessible area so students can refer to it during class discussions and other related activities. Next, distribute photocopies of the word finds on pages 120–121. Review the words in both word banks and add any to your class list that are not already included. Finally, have students complete their word finds. Afterward, tell them that they will use words from each puzzle in the creative writing assignment shown at the bottom of that page.

FARM ANIMAL REPORTS

Inspire some science-based inquiry into farm life with this activity. First, distribute a photocopy of the report sheet (page 122) to each student. Explain that students will choose a farm animal to research, using classroom or library books, the Internet, or other sources. Have them use their findings to fill out their report. (You might encourage students to search for information about their animal that is unknown to other class members or that will help to expand their knowledge base.) After students complete their reports, invite them to share their findings with the class. Then gather and bind the reports together to create a collaborative class book about farm animals.

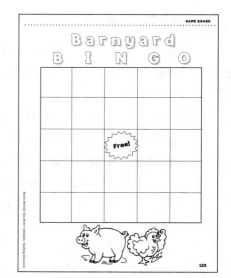

★ BARNYARD BINGO

Reinforce farm-related vocabulary words with a game of Bingo! To prepare, make several photocopies of the game board on page 123. On each page, fill in the vocabulary words you want students to practice, using the same words but in a different arrangement on each game board. (You might use words from the list created in "Farm Word Finds" on page 115.) Write each word on a plain index card. Copy the programmed game boards, making enough for each student in a group (or the whole class) to have one, then laminate. To use, supply players with Bingo chips or dried beans to use as markers, then have a caller choose one word card at a time to read to players. When players find that word on their game board, they cover it with a marker. Continue play until players have covered all of the words on their game boards. At that time, all the players call out "Bingo!" together.

★ FARM-FUN STORIES

 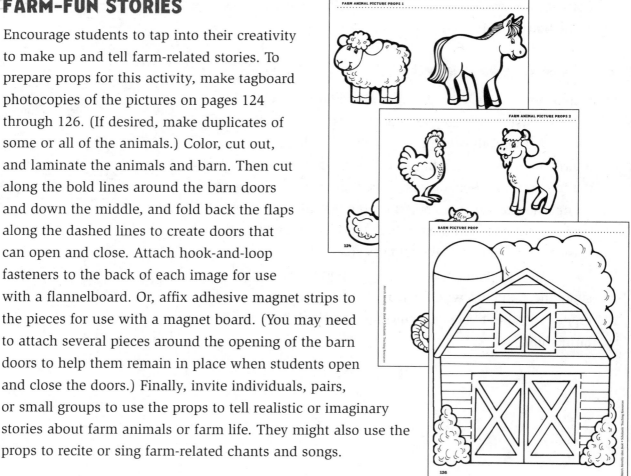

Encourage students to tap into their creativity to make up and tell farm-related stories. To prepare props for this activity, make tagboard photocopies of the pictures on pages 124 through 126. (If desired, make duplicates of some or all of the animals.) Color, cut out, and laminate the animals and barn. Then cut along the bold lines around the barn doors and down the middle, and fold back the flaps along the dashed lines to create doors that can open and close. Attach hook-and-loop fasteners to the back of each image for use with a flannelboard. Or, affix adhesive magnet strips to the pieces for use with a magnet board. (You may need to attach several pieces around the opening of the barn doors to help them remain in place when students open and close the doors.) Finally, invite individuals, pairs, or small groups to use the props to tell realistic or imaginary stories about farm animals or farm life. They might also use the props to recite or sing farm-related chants and songs.

★ HEN-AND-EGG NUMBER MATCH

Share with students that chicken farms are important because they produce nutritious eggs and poultry—two foods common to most households. Invite students to share about their favorite egg or chicken dish. Then use this activity to reinforce counting and number skills. To prepare, photocopy, color, and cut out a supply of the hen, nest, and egg patterns on page 127. Write a number on each hen and glue the corresponding number of eggs on a nest. For self-checking purposes, label the back of each nest with the number of eggs in that nest. Then laminate all of the pieces and place them in a learning center. Invite students to visit the center to match the hens and nests. Alternately, you might label each hen with a number word, or label the patterns with basic facts to give students practice with additional math skills.

★ FRESH FOODS FROM THE FARM

Tell students that many foods we enjoy at our tables come from both agricultural and animal farms. Work with the class to brainstorm a list of farm foods, such as corn, peas, strawberries, eggs, milk, beef, and fish. (You may want to explain to students that nowadays even fish are "farmed," meaning they are raised in special tanks.) Then photocopy the food cards on page 128. Color, cut out, and laminate the cards. Next, review each card with students, inviting them to discuss how that food is grown or where it comes from (such as from an animal). Later, to extend the activity, draw a T-chart on the chalkboard or on a whiteboard. On the left side, help students record some foods they had for lunch that day. On the right side, have them write about the connection each food has to a farm.

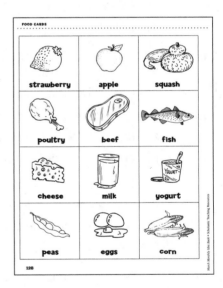

 # ★ FARM ANIMAL DRAMATIZATIONS

Write this favorite childhood chant on the chalkboard:

> This little piggy went to market.
>
> This little piggy stayed home.
>
> This little piggy had roast beef.
>
> This little piggy had none.
>
> And this little piggy cried
>
> "Wee-wee-wee!"
>
> All the way home.

Recite the chant with students. Then invite volunteers to repeat the chant, replacing "piggy" with a different farm animal name and "wee-wee-wee" with the sound that animal makes. For example, they might use "cow" and "moo-moo-moo" in the chant.

Next, distribute photocopies of the animal puppets (pages 129–131) and small paper bags to students. To make paper-bag puppets, ask students to color and cut out the patterns for each of their animals. Then have them glue the patterns to a paper bag to complete each puppet, as shown. Invite students to recite the chant about one of the animals while using the corresponding puppet as a prop.

If desired, challenge students to revise the chant even more by changing the animal name, sound, and actions in the lines. For example, they might revise the chant to the following:

> This little duck ate ice cream.
>
> This little duck ate pie.
>
> This little duck ate pizza.
>
> This little duck asked why.
>
> And this little duck cried
>
> "Quack-quack-quack!"
>
> As he flew into the sky.

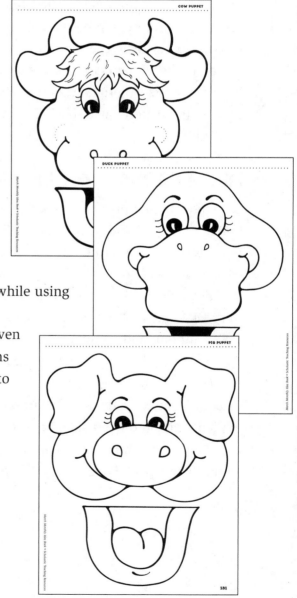

★ COWS AREN'T THE ONLY ONES!

Cows aren't the only mammals that provide milk for human consumption. Collect a number of animal resource books that feature milk-producing animals other than cows—such as goats, sheep, llamas, and camels. Explain that, while cow-milk is the most commonly used milk product in our country, milk can be used from several other animals. Show students pictures of other milk-producing animals. Tell them that all of these animals are mammals, then discuss the characteristics of each one.

Afterward, invite students to research cows to learn more about them. They might research a certain breed of cow, such as a Jersey, Holstein, or Guernsey, or research cows in general. Encourage students to use class or library books, the Internet, and other sources to gather facts and interesting information about their subject. After completing the final draft of their findings, have students make a cow page framer on which to display their written work. To make one, students color and cut out photocopies of the cow patterns on page 132. Then they glue the cow's head, legs, and tail to the edges of a 9- by 12-inch sheet of construction paper. Finally, they attach their writing to the page framer and display on a bulletin board.

★ FARM-FRESH PHRASES

Invite students to make up stories to explain the origins of some of the farm animal-related phrases below. Their stories can include factual information, imaginary events, or even humorous parts. Students can write their final copies on the stationery on page 133 and then bind their work to photocopies of their choice of covers on pages 134 and 135. To complete, have them color their cover and add a title and author line. Afterward, invite students to share their stories with the class.

bull-headed

chicken out

dog tired

got your goat

hog wash

hog wild

hold your horses

horse around

stubborn as a mule

talk turkey

On-the-Farm Word Find

Find these words in the puzzle below:

BOAR   BULL   COLT   DRAKE   EWE   GANDER

MARE   RAM   SILO   SOW   STALLION   SWINE

```
E C A L C S A R Z H A C O V B G E N O Y S T
B L E G A N D E R B A C S O U S F I D H G A
O N P I S R P M R O L S U N L S I N E O N W
U P C S T O L M J U T R S I L O N E W B O N
W I L O E U K U C C S O T H D K T N O O M T
B H A W P T E M O E R B X U R E R A M E R A
T X C O T S T A L L I O N C M R A I A R A X
N G L E L W N R T Z S A E D J S A P R N R E
F X O C V I O E C H D R A K E D L A E T E R
Q B U L B N B L O S S O M R W G D C V F G A
R P D X F E Y L X A R Y C H E H J K L P C A
N Z S M S D F A E T G D F Q A S W D K R G B
```

Using at least four words from the puzzle, tell about a farm that you have visited or read about in a book. If you need more space to write, use the back of this page.

_____

_____

_____

_____

March Monthly Idea Book © Scholastic Teaching Resources

Baby-Farm-Animal Word Find

Find these words in the puzzle below:

BUNNY   CALF   CHICK   DUCKLING   FOAL   GOSLING

KID   KITTEN   LAMB   PIGLET   PUPPY

```
E C A L C S A R Z H A C O V B G E N O Y S T
B L E G A N D E R B A C S O U S F I D H G A
O N P I S R R M R O L S B N L S I N E O N W
U P C S T P U P P Y T R U I L G N E W B O N
W I L O E U K I C C S O N H D W T D O O M T
B H A K P T E G O S L I N G R E R U M E R A
T X C O T S L L L I O Y C M R A C A L F X
N G L E L I N E T Z S A E D J S U K R A R E
F X O C V K I T T E N R A K F O A L E M E R
Q B U C H I C K O S S O M R X O Q I V B G A
R P D X F D Y L X A R Y C H E H J N L P C A
N Z S M S D F A E T G D F Q A S W G K R G B
```

Using at least four words from the puzzle, explain what farm animals you'd like to know more about and why. If you need more space to write, use the back of this page.

_____

_____

_____

_____

_____

Farm Animal Report

The name of my animal is:

_____

It is: ❏ a bird   ❏ a mammal   ❏ a reptile   ❏ an amphibian

This animal feeds on: _____

Some interesting facts about my animal are: _____

_____

_____

Here is a drawing of my animal!

March Monthly Idea Book © Scholastic Teaching Resources

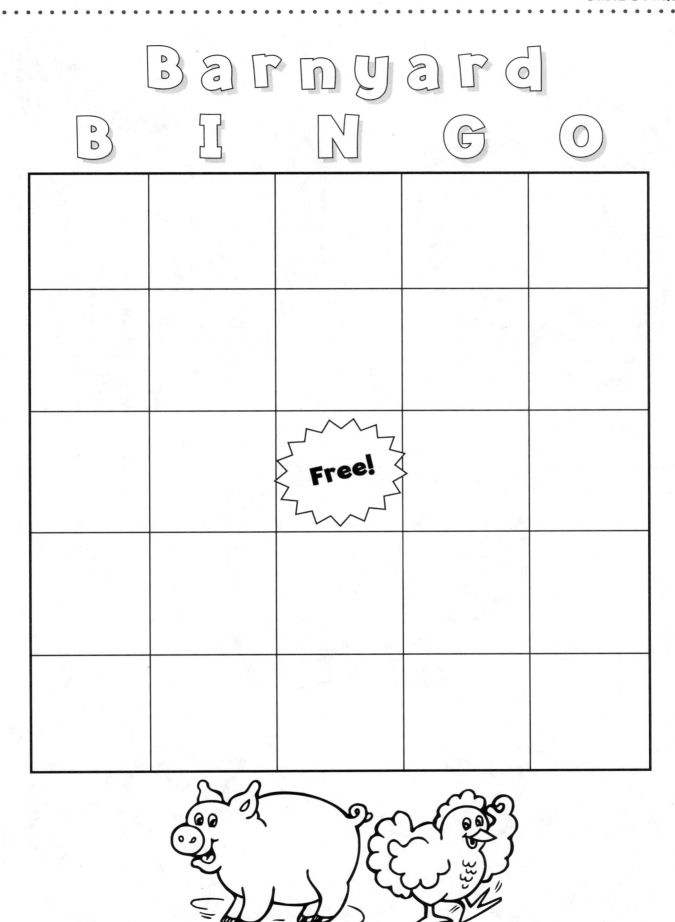

Barnyard
BINGO

Free!

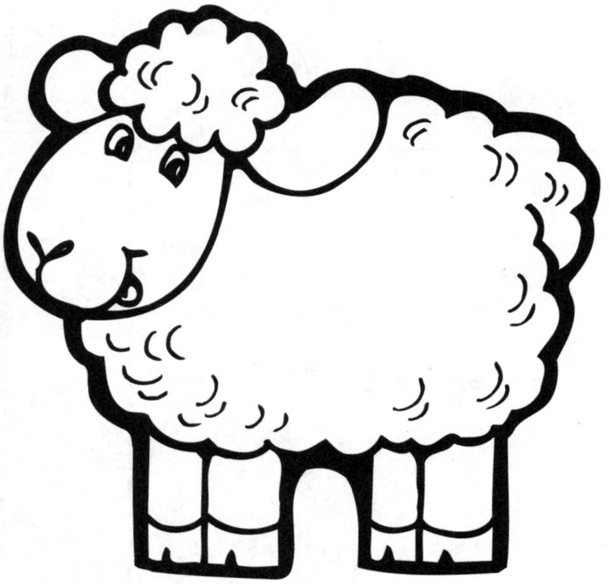

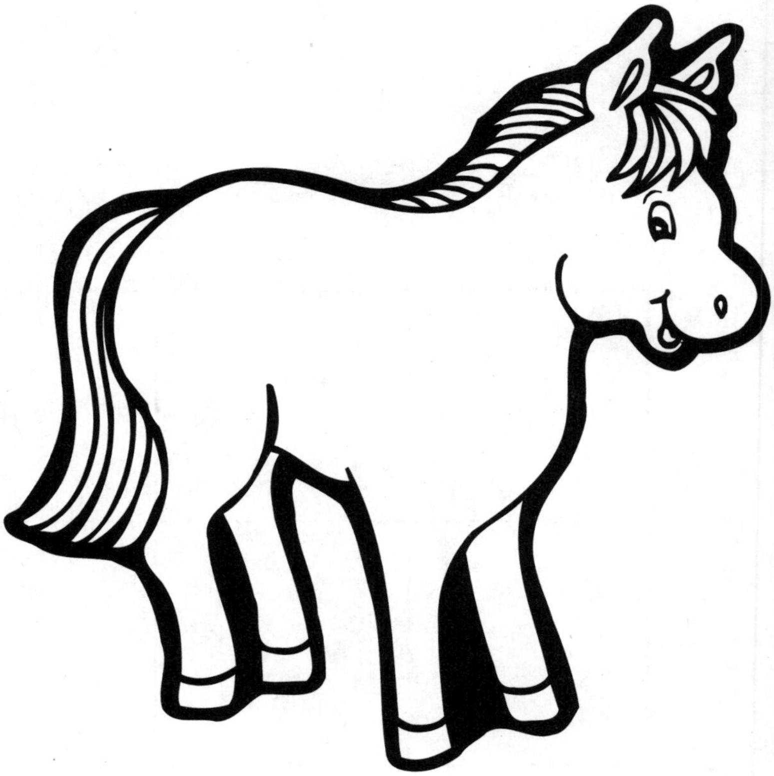

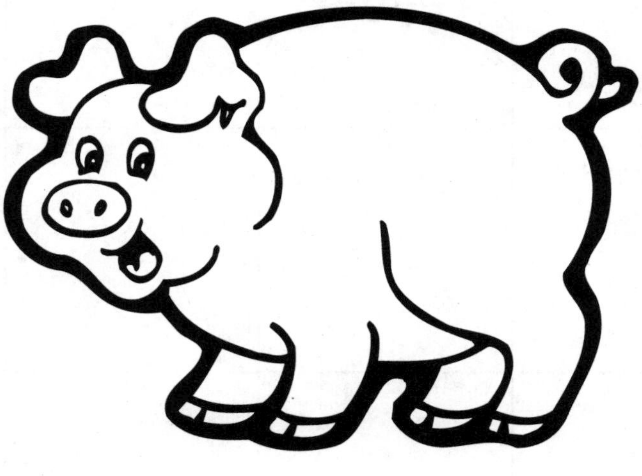

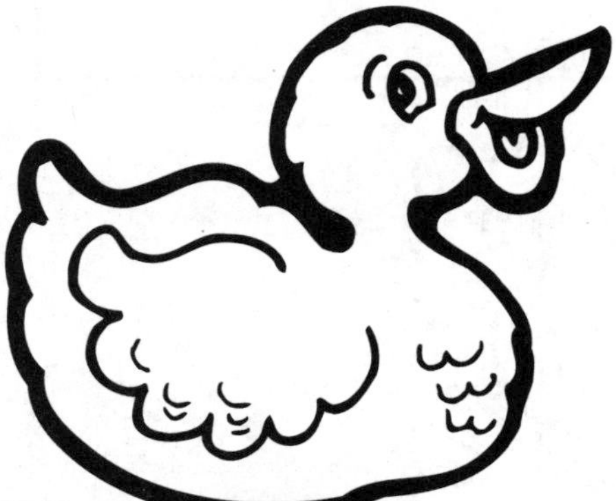

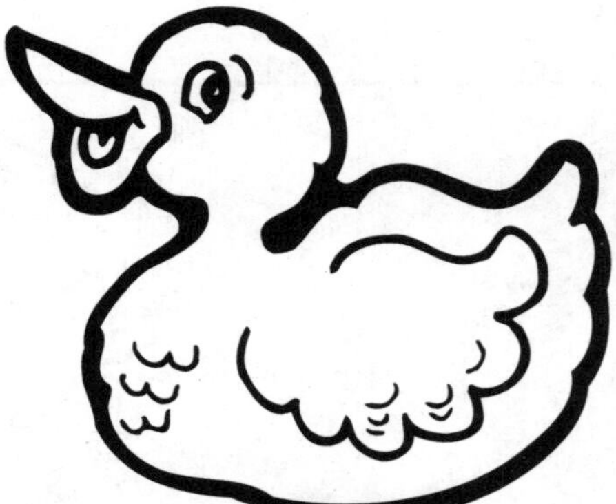

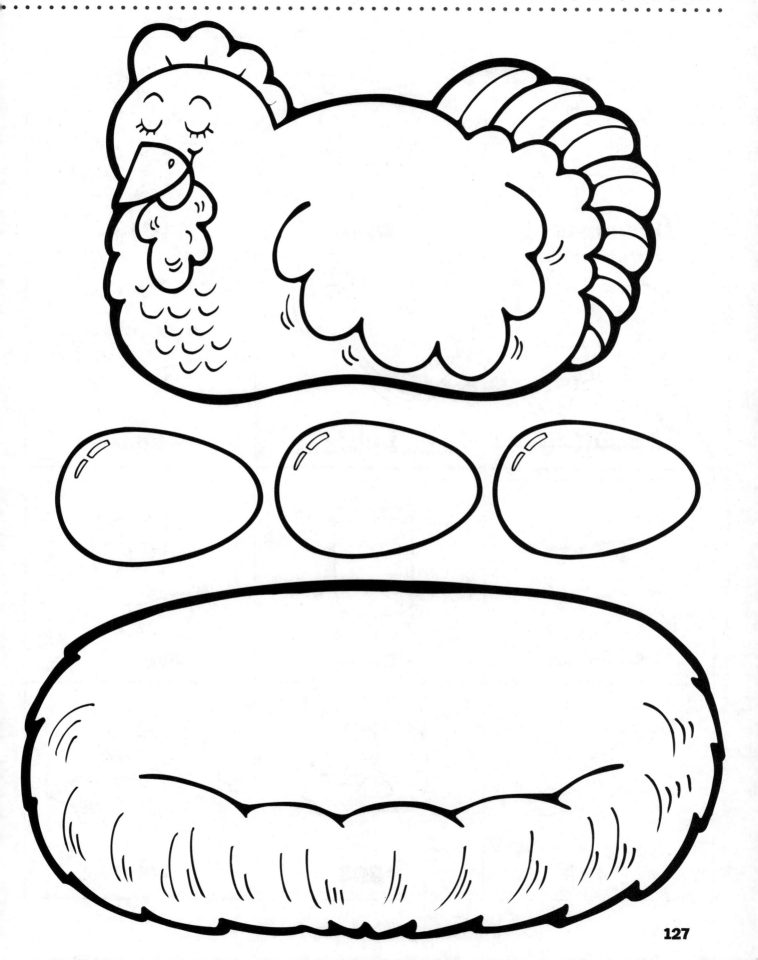

strawberry

apple

squash

poultry

beef

fish

cheese

milk

yogurt

peas

eggs

corn

AWARDS, INCENTIVES, AND MORE

Getting Started

Make several photocopies of the reproducibles on pages 138 through 142. Giving out the bookmarks, pencil toppers, notes, and certificates will show students your enthusiasm for their efforts and achievements. Plus, bookmarks and pencil toppers are a fun treat for students celebrating birthdays.

- Provide materials for decorating, including markers, color pencils, and stickers.

- Encourage students to bring home their creations to share and celebrate with family members.

★ BOOKMARKS

1. Photocopy onto tagboard and cut apart.

2. For more fanfare, punch a hole on one end and tie on a length of colorful ribbon or yarn.

★ PENCIL TOPPERS

1. Photocopy onto tagboard and cut out.

2. Use an art knife to cut through the Xs.

3. Slide a pencil through the Xs as shown.

SEND-HOME NOTES

1. Photocopy and cut apart.

2. Record the child's name and the date.

3. Add your signature.

4. Add more details about the student's day on the back of the note.

 ## CERTIFICATES

1. Photocopy.

2. Record the child's name and other information, as directed.

3. Add details about the child's achievement (if applicable), then add your signature and the date.

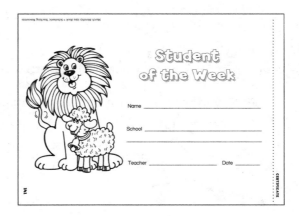

Read about . . .

Shamrocks

Leprechauns

Saint Patrick's Day

Rise and Shine by Reading a Book!

A Rainy Day Is a Book's Best Friend!

Student's Name

was a ray of sunshine today!

_____
Date

_____
Teacher

Student's Name

No "lion"— you did a great job!

_____   _____
Date   Teacher

Student's Name

was uplifting in class today!

_____   _____
Date   Teacher

Student's Name

was a real lamb in class today!

_____   _____
Date   Teacher

Student of the Week

Name _____

School _____

Teacher _____

Date _____

CERTIFICATE

Certificate of Achievement

Presented to

_____

Name

In recognition of _____

School _____

Teacher _____

Date _____

142

Irish Word Find, page 31

```
A M S D F R E T G D F Q A S W D F R G B N M C D S J
A L C M A R Z H A C O V B G E N J X N E O U K I G A
L E S D E F R T G J L D S H E N A N I G A N I L I T
R P D S H A M R O C K R H G H Y J U K N O L G T D U
P R F G T H Y J U D F R I G H Y N J U O N H Y U G A
I E W E D C V G T D E B L A R N E Y R M T S W A W O
L C X C V B G F D S A W L R T G R A D E O F R S E Y
X H A F R E T Y H G T R E D C J I G R A X R G H J S
G A E L I C X M Z S E R L V G Y N Y A R E F G V B N
X U C V B G T A I R E L A N D E R K L E R A S E D F
A N S D F R C Y A S D C G F G D C V F G A U W U S T
A S X F E Y R X A R Y C H B H J K L O P M N G F D S
```

Map of Japan, page 52

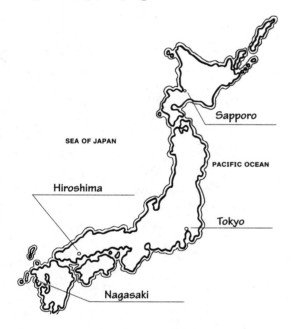

SEA OF JAPAN

PACIFIC OCEAN

Sapporo

Hiroshima

Tokyo

Nagasaki

Japanese Word Find, page 53

```
A M S D F R E T G D F Q A S W D K R G B N M C D S J
A L C M A R Z H A C O V B G E N O Y S T E R K I G A
L E K I T E R T G J L D S H Z F I N H G A N I L I T
R X I S O A M R O C S R H G H E J U R N O L G T D U
P R M G R H Y J U D F R I G H S N J I O N H Y U G A
I E O E I C V G T D T R A D I T I O N M T S W A W O
L C N C I B G F D S O W B R T I R A E E O F R S E Y
X L O T U S T Y H G R Z A D C V I T R A X R G H J S
G O E K I C X M Z S I R C V J A P A N R E F G V B N
X U C V B G T A H A I K U N D L A N T E R N S E D F
A N S D F R C Y A S D C S F G D C V F G A U W U S T
A S X F E Y R X A R Y C H B H J K L O P M N G F D S
```

Famous Women Word Find, page 77

```
S F R E T G B A R T O N D K R G B N M C D S
C M V R Z A C L V B G E N O C H O A R K I G
K I T E R G J V D S H E F I N H G A N I L I
R I S O R O C A D A M S E J U R N O L G T D
P R G Y J U D R R I G H B E T H U N E K U G
M E I V P E F E R A D I U I O N M T S W A W
L C C G E D S Z W B R T C R A Y E O F A S E
X L S T L H G R Q M I N K I T R P X R N H J
A X C L O C K W O O D J A P A N A E F G V B
U V B T S H A I K T N D L A N T R R N S E D
N F R I C E D C T F T D W A L K E R W U S
A S X F E Y R X A R Y C H B H O S M N F B P
```

Music Word Find, page 84

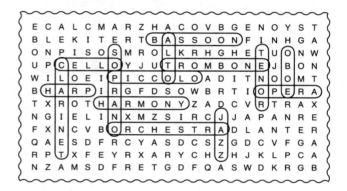

```
E C A L C M A R Z H A C O V B G E N O Y S T
B L E K I T E R T B A S S O O N F I N H G A
O N P I S O S M R O L K R H G H E T U O N W
U P C E L L O Y J U T R O M B O N E J B O N
W I L O E I P I C C O L O A D I T N O O M T
B H A R P I R G F D S O W B R T I O P E R A
T X R O T H A R M O N Y Z A D C V R T R A X
N G I E L I N X M Z S I R C J J A P A N R E
F X N C V B O R C H E S T R A D L A N T E R
Q A E S D F R C Y A S D C S Z G D C V F G A
R P T X F E Y R X A R Y C H Z H J K L P C A
N Z A M S D F R E T G D F Q A S W D K R G B
```

Unscramble each word. Write it on the line.

MRDU   DRUM

OPANI   PIANO

BTUA   TUBA

Spring Weather Word Find, page 100

```
E C A L C S A R Z H A C O V B W I N D Y S T
B L E K I P E R T B A C S O O S F I D H G A
O F P I S G S M R O L G U N S H V N J O N W
U A C S T O R M Y U T R O T B O N E W B O N
W I L O E L P U C O O L S H D W T N O O M T
B R A K P T E M P E R A T U R E I O P E R A
T X C O T S L B Y J U T R N M R A I N Y A X
N G L E L I N R M H O T U D J S A P A N R E
F X O C V B O M C H E S T E A D L A M T E R
Q S U L B F B I O Z S O M R E G D C V F G A
R P D X F E Y L X A R Y C H Z H J K L P C A
N Z Y M S R F D E T G D F Q A S U N N Y G B
```

Spring Quote Decoder, page 101

M A R C H   C O M E S   I N
L I K E   A   L I O N   A N D
G O E S   O U T   L I K E
A   L A M B !

On-the-Farm Word Find, page 120

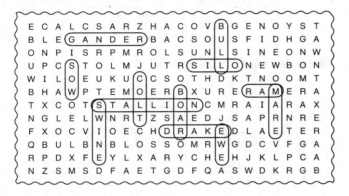

```
E C A L C S A R Z H A C O V B G E N O Y S T
B L E G A N D E R B A C S O U S F I D H G A
O N P I S R P M R O L S U N L S I N E O N W
U P C S T O L M J U T R S I L O N E W B O N
W I L O E U K U C C S O T H D K T N O O M T
B H A W P T E M O E R B X U R E R A M E R A
T X C O T S T A L L I O N C M R A I A R A X
N G L E L W N R T Z S A E D J S A P R N R E
F X O C V I O E C H D R A K E D L A E T E R
Q B U L B N B L O S S O M R W G D C V F G A
R P D X F E Y L X A R Y C H E H J K L P C A
N Z S M S D F A E T G D F Q A S W D K R G B
```

Baby-Farm-Animal Word Find, page 121

```
E C A L C S A R Z H A C O V B G E N O Y S T
B L E G A N D E R B A C S O U S F I D H G A
O N P I S R R M R O L S B N L S I N E O N W
U P C S T P U P P Y T R U I L G N E W B O N
W I L O E U K I C C S O N H D W T D O O M T
B H A K P T E G O S L I N G R E R U M E R A
T X C O T S T L L L I O Y C M R A C A L F X
N G L E L I N E T Z S A E D J S U K R A R E
F X O C V K I T T E N R A K F O A L E M E R
Q B U C H I C K O S S O M R X O Q I V B G A
R P D X F D Y L X A R Y C H E H J N L P C A
N Z S M S D F A E T G D F Q A S W G K R G B
```